PowerPoint Essentials

M.L. HUMPHREY

SELECT TITLES BY M.L. HUMPHREY

WORD ESSENTIALS
Word for Beginners
Intermediate Word

POWERPOINT ESSENTIALS
PowerPoint for Beginners
Intermediate PowerPoint

EXCEL ESSENTIALS
Excel for Beginners
Intermediate Excel
50 Useful Excel Functions
50 More Excel Functions

ACCESS ESSENTIALS
Access for Beginners
Intermediate Access

BUDGETING FOR BEGINNERS
Budgeting for Beginners
Excel for Budgeting

CONTENTS

PowerPoint for Beginners

POWERPOINT ESSENTIALS BOOK 1

M.L. HUMPHREY

CONTENTS

INTRODUCTION

The purpose of this guide is to introduce you to the basics of using Microsoft PowerPoint. If you've ever found yourself in a situation where you need to present to a larger audience than just a handful of people then you've probably needed PowerPoint. It's great for summarizing and organizing information and also the go-to software for creating presentation slides.

Of course, if you've ever been on the receiving end of a presentation made by a large consulting firm then you've probably seen how PowerPoint can be abused and misused to the point of ridiculousness. (Or is it just me that thinks that crowding a slide with so much information there's no way it could actually be legible if presented on a screen is wrong?)

Anyway. This guide will walk you through the basics of how to use PowerPoint. By the time you finish reading this guide you will be fully capable of creating a basic PowerPoint presentation that includes text, pictures, and/or tables of information. You will also be able to format any text you enter and will know how to add notes to your slides, animate your slides so that each bullet point appears separately, and launch your presentation as a slide show or print a copy or handouts.

(And, yes, this guide will even allow you to create overly-crowded dense slides with too much information on them if that's really what you want to do.)

As you can see, I will also be sprinkling in my opinion throughout this guide so it isn't just going to be how to do things in PowerPoint but why you might want to do it in a certain way.

There are other aspects to PowerPoint that I'm not going to cover in this guide. For example, we're not going to discuss how to use SmartArt.

The goal of this guide is to give you enough information on how to create a basic presentation without overwhelming you with information you may not need. I do, however, end with a discussion of your help options for learning more should you need it.

This guide is written using PowerPoint 2013. If you have a version of PowerPoint prior to 2007 your interface will look very different from mine. At this point, it's probably worth paying to upgrade to a more recent version of Office for anyone using a pre-2007 version, but that's up to you. If you do stick with an older version of PowerPoint, you'll be limited in terms of the resources you can find to help you when you get stuck. (Also the themes that will be discussed in this guide may not exist in your version.)

If you've already read *Word for Beginners* or *Excel for Beginners*, some portions of this guide will be familiar to you because the text options in PowerPoint work much the same way they do in Word and Excel. Also, the PowerPoint interface is structured in much the same way as both Word and Excel. If you're familiar with one of those programs already you should find PowerPoint easier to learn than someone who is new to all three.

Alright then. Now that you know what this guide is going to cover, let's get started with some basics.

BASIC TERMINOLOGY

Before we get started, I want to make sure that we're on the same page in terms of terminology. Some of this will be standard to anyone talking about these programs and some of it is my personal quirky way of saying things, so best to skim through if nothing else.

Tab

I refer to the menu choices at the top of the screen (File, Home, Insert, Design, Transitions, Animations, Slide Show, Review, and View) as tabs. If you click on one you'll see that the way it's highlighted sort of looks like an old-time filing system.

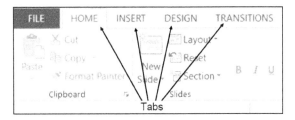

Each tab you select will show you different options. For example, in the image above, I have the Home tab selected and you can do various tasks such as cut/copy/paste, add new slides, change the slide layout, change fonts or font size or font color, change text formatting, add shapes, find/replace, etc. Other tabs give other options.

Click

If I tell you to click on something, that means to use your mouse (or trackpad) to move the arrow on the screen over to a specific location and left-click or right-click on the option. (See the next definition for the difference between left-click and right-click).

If you left-click, this selects the item. If you right-click, this generally creates a dropdown list of options to choose from. If I don't tell you which to do, left- or right-click, then left-click.

Left-click/Right-click

If you look at your mouse or your trackpad, you generally have two flat buttons to press. One is on the left side, one is on the right. If I say left-click that means to press down on the button on the left. If I say right-click that means press down on the button on the right.

Now, as I sadly learned when I had to upgrade computers, not all trackpads have the left- and right-hand buttons. In that case, you'll basically want to press on either the bottom left-hand side of the trackpad or the bottom right-hand side of the trackpad. Since you're working blind it may take a little trial and error to get the option you want working. (Or is that just me?)

Select or Highlight

If I tell you to select text, that means to left-click at the end of the text you want to select, hold that left-click, and move your cursor to the other end of the text you want to select.

Another option is to use the Shift key. Go to one end of the text you want to select. Hold down the shift key and use the arrow keys to move to the other end of the text you want to select. If you arrow up or down, that will select an entire row at a time.

With both methods, which side of the text you start on doesn't matter. You can start at the end and go to the beginning or start at the beginning and go to the end. Just start at one end or the other of the text you want to select.

The text you've selected will then be highlighted in gray.

If you need to select text that isn't touching you can do this by selecting your first section of text and then holding down the Ctrl key and selecting your second section of text using your mouse. (You can't arrow to the second section of text or you'll lose your already selected text.)

Dropdown Menu

If you right-click on a PowerPoint slide, you will see what I'm going to refer to as a dropdown menu. (Sometimes it will actually drop upward if you're towards the bottom of the document.)

A dropdown menu provides you a list of choices to select from like this one that you'll see if you right-click on a Title Slide in a presentation:

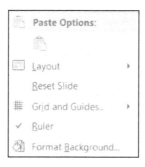

There are also dropdown menus available for some of the options listed under the tabs at the top of the screen. For example, if you go to the Home tab, you'll see small arrows below or next to some of the options, like the Layout option and the Section option in the Slides section. Clicking on those little arrows will give you a dropdown menu with a list of choices to choose from like this one for Layout:

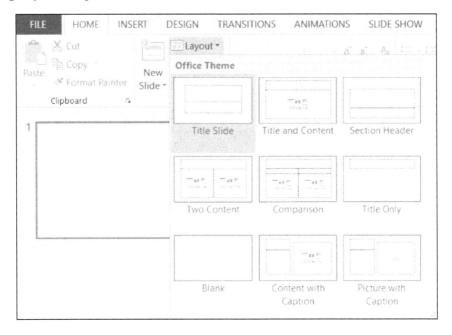

Expansion Arrows

I don't know the official word for these, but you'll also notice at the bottom right corner of most of the sections in each tab that there are little arrows. If you click on one of those arrows PowerPoint will bring up a more detailed set of options, usually through a dialogue box (which we'll discuss next).

In the Home tab, for example, there are expansion arrows for Clipboard, Font, Paragraph, and Drawing. Holding your mouse over the arrow will give a brief description of what clicking on the expansion arrow will do like here for the Clipboard section on the Home tab:

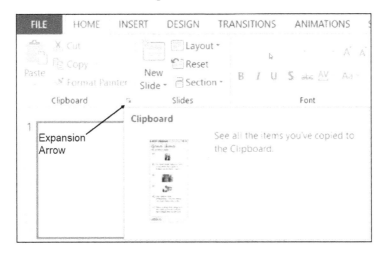

Dialogue Box

Dialogue boxes are pop-up boxes that cover specialized settings. As just mentioned, if you click on an expansion arrow, it will often open a dialogue box that contains more choices than are visible in that section. When you right-click on a PowerPoint content slide and choose Font, Paragraph, or Hyperlink that also opens dialogue boxes.

Dialogue boxes often allow the most granular level of control over an option. For example, this is the Font dialogue box which you can see has more options available than in the Font section of the Home tab.

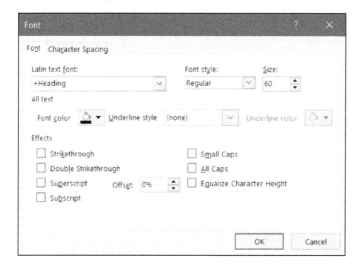

Scroll Bar

PowerPoint has multiple scroll bars that are normally visible. One is on the right-hand side of the slides that are displayed to the left of your screen (but only when there are enough slides to require scrolling). The other is on the right-hand side of the current slide that you're viewing in the main display section of PowerPoint when there are at least two slides in your presentation.

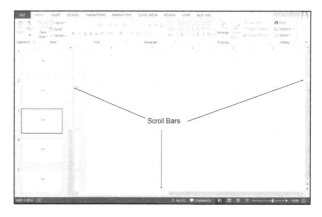

You can either click in the space above or below the scroll bar to move up or down a small amount or you can left-click on the bar, hold the left-click, and drag the bar up or down to move more quickly. You can also use the arrows at the top and the bottom to move up and down through your document.

In the default view where you can see an entire slide in the main screen, the right-hand scroll bar will move you through your presentation. Clicking on the scroll bar for the left-hand pane will keep you on the current slide but show you other slides in the presentation. (That you can then click on if you want to go to that slide.)

I generally use the scroll bar on the left-hand side when I use one at all.

You won't normally see a scroll bar at the bottom of the screen, but it is possible. This would happen if you ever change the zoom level to the point that you're not seeing the entire presentation slide on the screen. (To test this, click on the main slide, go to the View tab, click on Zoom, and choose 400%. You should now see a scroll bar on the bottom of the main section where your current slide is visible.)

Arrow

If I ever tell you to arrow to the left or right or up or down, that just means use your arrow keys. This will move your cursor to the left one space, to the right one space, up one line, or down one line. If you're at the end of a line and arrow to the right, it will take you to the beginning of the next line. If you're at the beginning of a line and arrow to the left, it will take you to the end of the last line.

Cursor

There are two possible meanings for cursor. One is the one I just used. When you're clicked into a PowerPoint slide, you will see that there is a blinking line. This indicates where you are in the document. If you type text, each letter will appear where the cursor was at the time you typed it. The cursor will move (at least in the U.S. and I'd assume most European versions) to the right as you type. This version of the cursor should be visible at all times unless you have text selected.

The other type of cursor is the one that's tied to the movement of your mouse or trackpad. When you're typing, it will not be visible. But stop typing and move your mouse or trackpad, and you'll see it. If the cursor is positioned over your text, it will look somewhat like a tall skinny capital I. If you move it up to the menu options or off to the sides, it becomes a white arrow. (Except for when you position it over any option under the tabs that can be typed in such as Font Size or Font where it will once again look like a skinny capital I.)

Usually I won't refer to your cursor, I'll just say, "click" or "select" or whatever action you need to take with it, and moving the cursor to that location will be implied.

Quick Access Toolbar

In the very top left corner of your screen when you have PowerPoint open you should see a series of symbols. These are part of the Quick Access Toolbar.

You can customize what options appear here by clicking on the downward pointing arrow with a line above it that you see at the very end of the list and then clicking on the commands you want to have available there. (If you don't want a command available, do the same thing. Click on the dropdown arrow and then click on the command so it's no longer selected.) Selected commands have a checkmark next to them.

The Quick Access Toolbar can be useful if there's something you're doing repeatedly that's located on a different tab than something else you're doing repeatedly. I, for example, have customized my toolbar in Word to allow me to easily insert section breaks without having to move away from the Home tab.

To see what command a symbol in your toolbar represents, hold your cursor over the symbol.

Control Shortcuts

Throughout this document, I'm going to mention various control shortcuts that you can use to perform tasks like save, copy, cut, and paste. Each of these will be written as Ctrl + a capital letter, but when you use the shortcut on your computer you don't need to use the capitalized version of the letter. For example, holding down the Ctrl key and the s key at the same time will save your document. I'll write this as Ctrl + S, but that just means hold down the key that says ctrl and the s key at the same time.

Undo

One of the most powerful control shortcuts in PowerPoint (or any program, really) is the Undo option. If you do something you didn't mean to or that you want to take back, use Ctrl + Z to undo it. This should step you back one step and reverse whatever you just did. If you need to reverse more than one step, just keep using Ctrl + Z until you've undone everything you wanted to undo.

(There is also a small left-pointing arrow in the Quick Access Toolbar that will do the same thing.)

ABSOLUTE BASICS

Now let's discuss some absolute basics, like opening, closing, saving, and deleting presentations.

Starting a New PowerPoint Presentation

To start a brand new PowerPoint presentation, I click on PowerPoint 2013 from my applications menu or the shortcut I have on my computer's taskbar. If you're already in PowerPoint and want to open a new PowerPoint presentation you can go to the File tab and choose New from the left-hand menu.

Any of these options will bring up a list of various presentation themes you can choose from. I usually use one of these when I'm doing a non-corporate presentation rather than try to create a presentation from scratch.

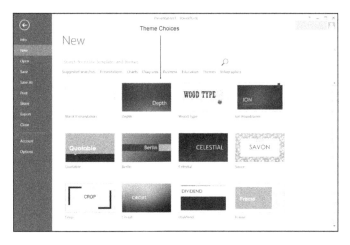

Clicking on any of the themes will bring up a secondary display where you can then use the "More Images" arrows at the bottom to see what the various slides in the presentation will look like. With most of these options you can also click on variant versions that are shown to the right side that are generally the same in terms of layout and font but provide different color options.

For example, the Vapor Trail theme has two options with a black background and two with a white background.

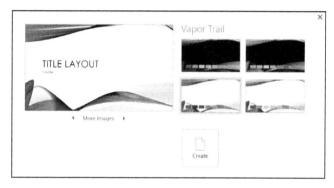

Once you find a template that you like click on Create and PowerPoint will open a new presentation for you that has the Title Slide for that template shown.

As you choose which theme you're going to use, I'd encourage you to think of your potential audience and which presentation is most appropriate for that audience. For example, I personally like the look of Vapor Trail but I would never use it for a presentation to one of my corporate clients. It's too artistic for that audience and the type of consulting I do.

If you have a company-provided template it's best to open that template (discussed next) and work from there.

You can also use Ctrl + N to start a new presentation but that will bring up a Title Slide that has no theme and is just plain white. (You can then choose a theme from the Design tab in PowerPoint as we'll discuss later.)

Opening an Existing PowerPoint File

To open an existing PowerPoint file you can go to the folder where the file is saved and double-click on the file name. Or you can open PowerPoint without selecting a file and it will provide a list of recent documents to choose from on the left-hand side of the screen.

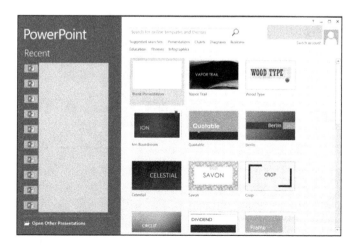

There is also an option at the bottom of that list of recent files to Open Other Presentations. If you click on that it will take you to the Open option that is normally available under the File tab. If you're already in PowerPoint you can access this option by going to the File tab and choosing Open from the left-hand menu or using Ctrl + O.

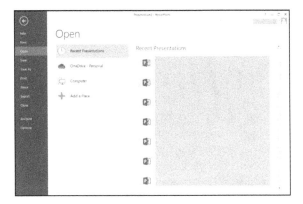

If the document you need is listed, left-click on it once and it will open. (As long as you haven't renamed the file or moved it since it was last opened. In that case, you'll need to navigate to where the file is saved and open it that way, either within PowerPoint or outside of PowerPoint.)

If the document you need is not listed in the list of Recent Presentations or has been moved or renamed since it was last used, click on Computer. (Or OneDrive if you store files in the cloud.) You can then navigate to the folder where the file you need is saved by either clicking on the folder name under Current Folder or Recent Folders (if listed) or by clicking on Browse to bring up the Open dialogue box.

Saving a PowerPoint File

To quickly save your presentation, you can use Ctrl + S or click on the small image of a floppy disk in the top left corner of the screen above File. For a document you've already saved that will overwrite the prior version of the document with the current version and will keep the file name, file type, and file location the same.

If you try to save a file that has never been saved before, it will automatically default to the Save As option which requires that you specify where to save the file, give it a name, and designate the file type. There are defaults for name and format, but you'll want to change the name of the document to something better than Document2.

You can also choose Save As when you want to change the location of a file, the name of a file, or the file type. (With respect to file type, I sometimes need to, for example, save a presentation file as a .pdf file or a .jpg file instead.) To do so, go to File and choose Save As from there.

The first choice you have to make for Save As is where you want to save the file. I see a list of my most recent seven folders listed and can also choose to Browse if I want to use a different location than one of the folders listed.

When you click on the location where you want to save the file, this will bring up the Save As dialogue box. Type in the name you want for the file and choose the file type. My file type defaults to PowerPoint Presentation (.pptx), but that can be changed using the dropdown next to "Save as type."

If you had already saved the file and you choose to Save As but keep the same location, name, and format as before, PowerPoint will overwrite the previous version of the file just like it would have if you'd used Save.

If you just want to rename a file, it's actually best to close the file and then go to where the file is saved and rename it that way rather than use Save As. Using Save As will keep the original of the file as well as creating the newer version. That's great when you want version control (which is rarely needed for PowerPoint), but not when you just wanted to rename your file from Great Presentation v22 to Great Presentation FINAL.

Renaming a PowerPoint File

As discussed above, you can use Save As to give an existing file a new name, but that approach will leave you with two versions of the file, one with the old name and one with the new name. If you just want to change the name of the existing file, close it and then navigate to where you've saved it. Click on the file name once to select it, click on it a second time to highlight the name, and then type in the new name you want to use, replacing the old one. If you rename the file this way outside of PowerPoint, there will only be one version of the file left, the one with the new name you wanted.

Just be aware that if you rename a file by navigating to where it's located and changing the name you won't be able to access the file from the Recent Presentations list under Open since that will still list the old name which no longer exists.

Deleting a PowerPoint File

You can't delete a PowerPoint file from within PowerPoint. You need to close the file you want to delete and then navigate to where the file is stored and delete the file there without opening it. Once you've located the file, click on the file name. (Only enough to select it. Make sure you haven't double-clicked and highlighted the name which will delete the file name but not the file.) Next, choose Delete from the menu at the top of the screen, or right-click and choose Delete from the dropdown menu.

Closing a PowerPoint File

To close a PowerPoint file click on the X in the top right corner or go to File and then choose Close. (You can also use Ctrl + W, but I never have.)

If no changes have been made to the document since you saved it last, it will just close.

If changes have been made, PowerPoint should ask you if you want to save those changes. You can either choose to save them, not save them, or cancel closing the document and leave it open. I almost always default to saving any changes. If I'm in doubt about whether I'd be overwriting something important, I cancel and choose to Save As and save the current file as a later version of the document just in case (e.g., Great Presentation v2).

If you had copied an image or a large block of text, you may also have a box pop up asking if you want to keep that image or text when you close the document. Usually the answer to this is no, but if you had planned on pasting that image or text somewhere else and hadn't yet done so, you can say to keep it on the clipboard.

YOUR WORKSPACE

Whether you choose to start a brand new file or open an existing file, you'll end up in the main workspace for PowerPoint. It looks something like this:

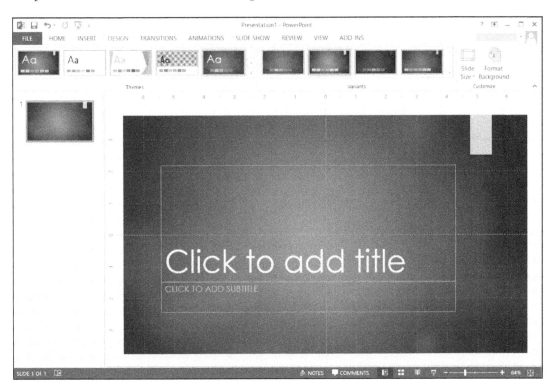

We'll walk through this in more detail in the *Working with Your Presentation Slides* section but I just wanted you to see right now that there's a left-hand pane that shows all of the slides in the presentation and then a main section of the screen that shows the slide you're currently working on.

For a new presentation there's just the one slide.

* * *

For a fully-built presentation, it will look more like this:

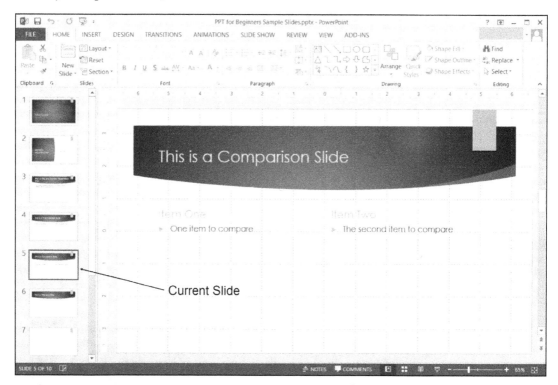

The slide you're currently seeing in the main section of the screen will have a dark border around it in the left-hand pane and your slides will be numbered starting at 1.

Across the top are your menu tabs and there are scroll bars for both the left-hand pane and the main section as well. Along the bottom are a couple of additional pieces of information or settings, including a zoom option in the bottom right corner.

CHOOSING A
PRESENTATION THEME

If you use Ctrl + N to start a new presentation you will have a blank presentation with no design elements. As a beginner, I would suggest that you use one of the PowerPoint designs for your presentation rather than create a design from scratch. (And the rest of this guide assumes that's the choice you're going to make. I do not cover in this guide how to build a presentation from scratch. That's intermediate-level.)

Also, sometimes you're going to choose a theme when you start a new presentation and then decide that that design doesn't work for your purposes and want to change it.

It's very easy to switch between design themes in PowerPoint, so let's walk through how to do it.

Open the presentation you want to change.

Go to the Design tab.

You should see that the Themes section takes up most of the screen.

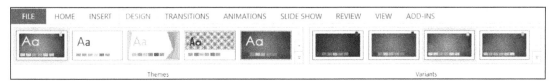

The far left-hand thumbnail in that section is your current design template.

On the right-hand side of the Design tab you'll see a separate section titled Variants.

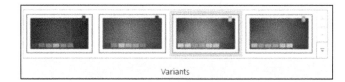

This will show different color variations on your current theme. So with the Ion theme if I wanted a purple background instead of a blue one, I could click on that image in the Variant section to change my presentation.

The rest of the thumbnails in the Themes section are other design templates you can choose from.

I would recommend having a Title and Content Slide visible in your presentation and using that to decide. (Right-click in the left-hand pane and choose New Slide to add one.) The reason for this is that some of the design templates put the header section of the slide at the bottom instead of the top. Or they have a colored background on all of the slides instead of just the Title Slide. You'll want to know that before you choose that theme since it can significantly impact the effectiveness of your presentation.

(My recommendation would be to choose a theme with a white background for the main slides and with the title section at the top. At least for standard corporate presentations.)

To see what your slides will look like before you change the theme, just hold your cursor over each thumbnail image in the Theme section of the Design tab and the slide in the main screen will change to show that theme.

To select that theme, click on the thumbnail image. All of your slides should then change over to the new theme and that thumbnail should now be visible as the left-most thumbnail in the Theme section.

(If you are using sections in your presentation, something we won't cover in this guide, then only the slides in your current section will change to the new theme. So using sections would be a way to use multiple themes in a single presentation, although I wouldn't recommend doing that. The point of using a design theme is that it provides cohesiveness to a presentation.)

POWERPOINT SLIDE TYPES

There are a number of slide types available to you in PowerPoint. Probably more than you'll actually need. But I wanted to run through them real quick before we go any further because I'm going to occasionally refer to a slide type and I want you to know what I'm talking about when I do so.

The images below use the Ion Boardroom theme. If you want to change the slide type of a slide, you can right-click on that slide, go to Layout, and choose from the listed options there. Not all themes or templates will have all slide types in them. And different themes may have the elements in different locations on the slide. For example, some put the header at the bottom instead of the top.

You can put together a perfectly adequate presentation with just the Title Slide, Section Header, and Title and Content slide types, but I'll walk through most of the others for you just in case.

Title Slide

The Title slide is the default first slide for a presentation. It has a section for adding a title and a subtitle and, if you choose one of the templates provided in PowerPoint, a background that covers the rest of the slide and matches your chosen theme.

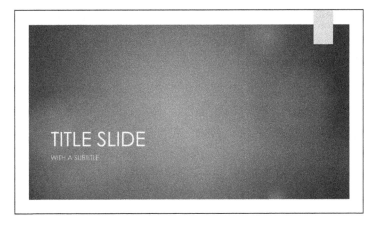

Section Header

If you are going to have sections within your presentation, then you'll want to separate them using a Section Header slide. Like the title slides above this slide will have a colored background that matches your theme. It will generally have the text in a different position or using a different font or font size to distinguish it from the title slide or will use a different color for the background or move the background image to a new location.

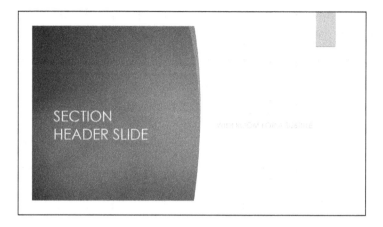

Title and Content Slide

The Title and Content slide is the one I use for most of my presentations. It has a section where you can describe what the slide is discussing and then a content box where you can add text, images, etc. When you're doing a basic presentation with a bulleted set of talking points, this is the slide that you'll probably use the most often.

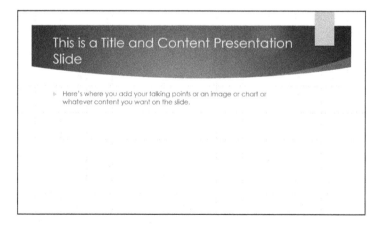

While most themes will have the title portion at the top (and I think that's the best choice for a corporate presentation) some of the themes have the title portion at the bottom or off to the side, so check your theme before you choose it. For example, this is the Title and Content Slide from the Slice theme using the exact same text as the image above.

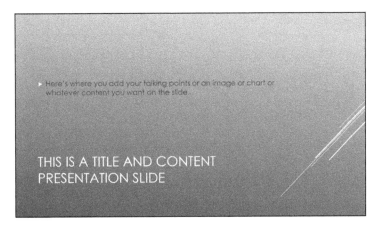

As you can also see above, content slides will sometimes have a colored background and sometimes will not depending on the theme you choose. Also, some themes use all caps in the title section and some do not. If you're switching between themes, be careful with this because it's easy with a theme that uses all caps to not pay attention to your capitalization and then move to a theme that uses upper and lower case and have some words capitalized and some not.

Two Content

The Two Content slide is another content slide. This slide has a section for a title and then two content boxes. It can be a good choice for when you want to either have two separate bulleted lists side by side or when you want to have text next to an image. You put the text in one of the boxes and the image in the other.

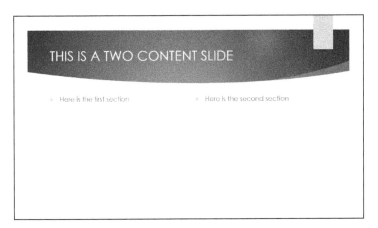

Comparison

The Comparison slide is also a content slide. It's much like the Two Content slide except it has added sections directly above each of the two text boxes where you can put header text to describe the contents of each of the boxes below.

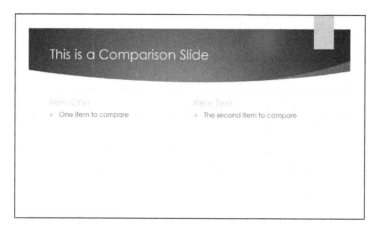

Title Only

The Title Only slide is a content slide that just has the title section and nothing else below it. You can add elements to the body of this slide, such as a text box or an image, but there is no pre-defined space for it like with the prior content slide types. It will have the same background as content slides for your selected theme.

Content With Caption

The Content With Caption slide is another content slide. In this one the title section covers half of the screen and there are two text boxes where you can add text, images, etc. One is below the title and the other takes up the other side of the slide.

Picture With Caption

The Picture With Caption slide is a slide you'd probably use for an appendix or some information you're calling out separate from the main presentation. It has a large section for a picture and then a section for title and text. (In the picture below I added a stock photo of some keyboard keys to the section for the photo and it took a portion of the image and scaled it to fit.)

Quote With Caption

The Quote With Caption slide is a slide that has quote marks around the main text section and then a smaller text box for an attribution of who said the quote as well as a larger text box for comments.

Blank

The blank slide has the same background as the other content slides for your chosen theme, but nothing else.

Other

Some themes will have even more pre-formatted slide types you can use. The Ion Boardroom theme has a three-column version as well as a few others I didn't cover here. And some won't have this many. If you need a specific slide type, be sure to check that that slide type is available before you get too far into working with your chosen theme.

WORKING WITH YOUR PRESENTATION SLIDES

In this chapter we're going to assume that you've created a brand new presentation using one of the templates. So now you find yourself in PowerPoint with a title slide visible on the left-hand side and in the main screen:

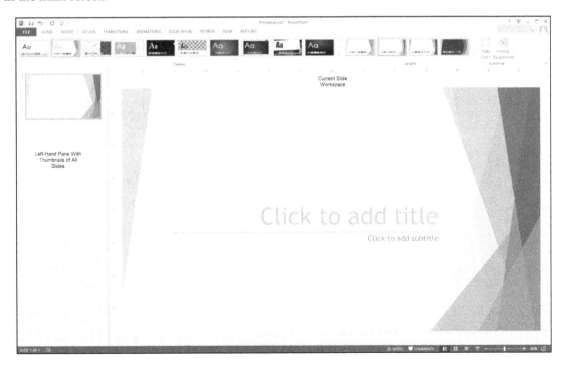

First things first, let's talk about what you're seeing. On the left-hand side of the screen are thumbnail (i.e., small) images of your slides. As you add new slides to your presentation they'll appear in this left-hand pane. In the center of the screen and taking up most of the space is the current slide you are working on. Because there's only this one slide to begin with it's going to be your title slide when you first open the file.

You can click on any of the slides in the left-hand pane or you can click on the slide in the center. Depending on which one you're clicked into, you'll be able to do different things such as add text to a slide or move a slide to a different location.

Let's start with the left-hand pane because that's where you'll work to change the positioning of your slides as well as add new ones or delete ones you no longer want.

If you right-click into the blank space below the title slide, you'll see that you have the option to add a new slide or add a new section. (In the hundreds of presentations I've done I've never needed to use sections so we're going to set that aside as an intermediate topic.) If you had copied slides from another presentation or even this one, you could also paste them as well, but since we haven't copied any slides yet that's not actually an available option. So all you have is the New Slide option.

If you choose that option, PowerPoint will insert a Title and Content slide for you. (Since this is the most common slide type I use for inputting information, it's convenient that PowerPoint defaults to that slide type.)

Now that we have two slides, let's discuss how you can select a slide or slides and how to move slides within your presentation.

Selecting a Slide or Slides

To select a single slide, you simply left-click on the slide where it's visible in the left-hand pane. When a slide is selected it should have a darker border around it. In my version of PowerPoint that border is red.

If you want to select more than once slide, you can select the first slide and then hold down the Ctrl key as you left-click on the next slide or slides that you want to select. When you do this each slide you click on will have that dark border around it.

Slides do not need to be next to one another for you to select them this way.

If you have a range of slides that you want to select, you can use the Shift key instead. Click on the slide at the top or the bottom of the range of slides you want, hold down the Shift key, and then click on the slide at the other end of the range of slides you want. All slides within that range, including the first slide you clicked and the second slide you clicked, should now have a dark border around them.

So, for example, if I want to select the first four slides in my presentation, I can click on the first slide, hold down the Shift key, and then click on the fourth slide. Or I could click on the fourth slide, hold down the Shift key, and then click on the first slide. As long as the slides you click on are at the beginning and end of your range of desired slides, you will select all of them.

(You can also combine methods of selecting slides to, for example, select a range of slides using Shift and then select an additional slide using the Ctrl key.)

No matter how many slides you select, the main screen will only show one of them.

To remove your selection of multiple slides, click in the gray area around any of the slides or on the main presentation slide.

Moving a Slide or Slides

The easiest way to move a slide or slides to a different position within your presentation is to select the slide(s) (as noted above) and then left-click and drag the slide(s) to the new location. As you move your chosen slide(s) you'll see the slides in the left-hand pane moving upward or downward to leave a space for your slides to be inserted. (It sounds weird, but just try it and you'll see what I'm talking about.)

If you've selected more than one slide, you can left-click on any of the slides you've selected and drag and all of the slides will move to the new location even if they weren't next to one another before.

Cutting a Slide or Slides

If you right-click on a slide or slides that you've selected and choose Cut from the dropdown menu, you can remove the slide or slides from their current location in the presentation. You can also do this by selecting the slide(s) and then using Ctrl + X.

Where cutting differs from deleting, which will have the same effect of removing the slides, is that cutting the slides allows you to move them elsewhere. You could cut them and then paste them into another location in that same presentation (using Paste which we'll discuss in a moment) or you could paste them into another PowerPoint presentation.

Cutting only deletes slides if you cut them and then choose not to put them in a new location.

Usually you can just select and drag slides into a new location within your presentation as we just discussed above, but if you have a very long presentation (say 200 slides) and want to move a slide from the beginning to the end, for example, it can be faster to cut the slide, scroll down to the end, and then paste.

You can also cut a slide by clicking on it, going to the Clipboard section of the Home tab, and choosing Cut from there.

Copying a Slide or Slides

If you right-click on a slide or slides that you've selected and choose Copy from the dropdown men, you can keep a version of the slides exactly where they were while creating a copy of those slides that you can then move into a new presentation or move to a new location within your existing presentation. (Using Paste which we'll discuss next.)

You can also use Ctrl + C to copy a set of slides. So select the slides you want to copy and then type Ctrl + C.

Where copy differs from cut is that it leaves the original version of the slides where they were. You now end up with two identical copies of that set of slides and you can place that second copy of the slides wherever you need them, either in your current presentation or another one.

(I tend to use Duplicate Slide instead when I'm working in a presentation. We'll talk about that one in a moment.)

You can also copy a slide by clicking on it, going to the Clipboard section of the Home tab, and choosing Copy from there.

Pasting a Slide or Slides

If you copy or cut a slide or slides and want to use them elsewhere, you need to paste them into that new location. You can do a basic paste by clicking into the space where you want to put those slides (so between two existing slides or in the gray space at the end of the presentation, for example) and using Ctrl + V.

If you are clicked onto a slide when you paste, your copied or cut slides will be pasted in below that slide.

You can also right-click where you want to paste a slide and choose from the paste options.

The first option, which has a small a in the bottom right corner, is Use Destination Theme. If you're cutting or copying and pasting within an existing presentation this won't mean much. But I've used this one often when working with a corporate PowerPoint template where someone drafted a presentation without using the corporate template and then handed it off to me and asked me to make it look like it should. (Always a pleasure when that happens.)

In those cases, I copy all of the slides from the version of the presentation I've been given and paste it into the corporate template using the destination theme option. This will convert the slides you pasted in from whatever theme they were using to your corporate template theme.

(You can test this for yourself by cutting a slide from your current presentation, changing the theme of your current presentation, and then right-clicking and pasting the slide back into your presentation using the Use Destination Theme option.)

Use Destination Theme is also what happens when you just use Ctrl + V.

The second paste option you have, the one with the paintbrush in the bottom right corner, is Keep Source Formatting. This does what it says, it keeps the formatting the slide(s) already had. Sometimes it's important to do this especially if you've done a lot of custom work on a slide and don't want your images, charts, etc. resized when you move them into a new presentation.

The third paste option, the one with a photo icon in the bottom right corner, is to paste a slide in as a Picture. That means the slide can no longer be edited. It's like someone took a snapshot of that slide and now you just have that snapshot. If you try to use this option with multiple slides only the first slide will paste in.

I would expect you won't use this one often.

You can also paste slides by going to the Clipboard section of the Home tab and choosing Paste from there. The more advanced options are available by clicking on the arrow under Paste.

Adding a New Slide

If you right-click on an existing slide in the presentation or in the gray area in the left-hand pane, you can add a new slide by choosing New Slide from the dropdown menu.

If you click on a slide and then choose New Slide, the slide that is added to your presentation will match the type of the slide you were clicked onto when you made that choice.

If you click in the gray area to add a slide, the slide type will match the slide directly above where you had clicked. (With the exception of a Title slide. In that case the new slide added will be a Title and Content slide.)

You can also go to the Slides section of the Home tab and click on New Slide there. If you use the dropdown arrow next to New Slide you can choose the layout for the new slide before you add it.

Duplicating a Slide

If you want to create a duplicate of an existing slide (something I do when I've created custom formatting and don't want to have to recreate it on each slide), you can right-click on a slide and choose Duplicate Slide. This will create an exact duplicate of the slide you right-clicked on.

You can also duplicate a slide by clicking on the slide, going to the Clipboard section of the Home tab, clicking on the arrow next to Copy, and choosing Duplicate from the dropdown menu.

Deleting a Slide

To delete a slide, you can click on that slide and then hit the Delete or Backspace key. Either one will work. Or you can right-click on that slide and choose Delete Slide from the dropdown menu.

Choosing the Slide Layout

To change the type of slide, select the slide or slides you need to change, right-click, go to Layout, and select the type you want from the available options. Each one will have the type listed as well as a small thumbnail image.

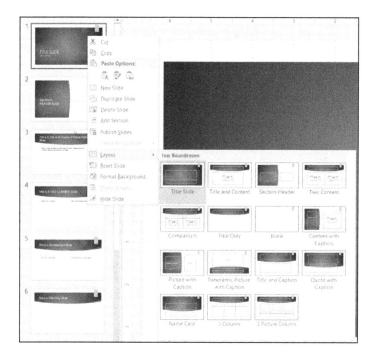

Different themes will have different options available. For example, the Ion theme has a Quote with Caption slide option that is not available in the Integral theme.

If you're using a custom theme (such as a corporate one) and don't have example slides in the presentation of the type you need, you may not have that layout option available to choose even though it exists in your corporate template. (This is why if I'm ever working with a corporate template I leave the sample slides in my presentation until I'm done and then delete them at the very last minute to make sure I won't need one of those choices.)

PowerPoint will do its best to change your current slide over to the chosen layout, but if you already had content in a slide when you changed the layout be sure to review each slide to make sure the way that PowerPoint changed the slide to the new layout makes sense.

You can also select a slide or slides, go to the Slides section of the Home tab, click on the dropdown arrow next to Layout, and choose your layout from there.

Resetting a Slide

If you makes changes to the layout of a slide, by for example changing the size of the text boxes or their location, and want to go back to the original layout for that slide type, you can right-click on the slide and choose Reset Slide from the dropdown menu. According to PowerPoint, this will "reset the position, size, and formatting of the slide placeholders to their default settings."

You can also click on a slide and go to the Slides section of the Home tab and choose Reset from there.

ADDING TEXT TO A PRESENTATION SLIDE

Now let's turn our attention from the left-hand pane to the main section of your PowerPoint screen where your current slide is shown.

Adding text to an existing slide is very simple. You click and type.

For example, here, is a Title slide:

You can see that the slide says "CLICK TO ADD TITLE" and "CLICK TO ADD SUBTITLE". And it's almost that easy. Click on where it say that and type. Click away when you're done. You will now be able to see whatever text you typed in that space and formatted according to that theme. (Usually that will cover text color and whether the text appears in all caps or not.)

If you add a different type of slide, such as a Title and Content slide, you'll see that that slide also has sections for adding text. It says "CLICK TO ADD TITLE" and "CLICK TO ADD TEXT". Many of the themes are pre-formatted to create bulleted lists that match the theme. As soon as you type, your text will be shown as part of a bulleted list. And each time you hit Enter a new bullet point will appear.

If you need to create subpoints, use the tab key to indent the line before you start typing your text. In some templates this will also change the type of bullet used or change the size of the bullet.

If you need to remove an indent, use Shift+Tab before your start typing.

For lines that have already been added where you need to adjust the indent, click to the left of the first letter in that line and then use Tab or Shift + Tab to adjust the indent. You can also use the Decrease List Level and Increase List Level options in the Paragraph section of the Home tab. They're the ones with lines with an arrow pointing either left or right in the middle of the top row.

By default the PowerPoint themes use fonts and font sizes that are legible for a presentation given on a projector. But the slides are also dynamic in the sense that as you add more and more and more to a slide the text in that slide will adjust in size to fit in the text box on the slide. Be careful with this.

For two reasons. First, if you let the font size get too small, no one will be able to read your slide. Why put together a presentation that no one can read?

Second, because this can happen on a slide-by-slide basis it can create a disjointed presentation. If one slide has bullet points in a 20 point size and another has bullet points in a 14 point size and another has them in an 11 point size, even if the font and colors are consistent across slides it can be jarring.

I try when I can to make the font size consistent across slides. So if I do have a very busy slide that requires a smaller font size than the default, then I'll usually change all other slides in the presentation to match that font size. (Easier to simplify the language instead, but that's not always an option when working on group projects.)

Be especially careful about legibility with respect to your subpoints. Each level of subpoint generally uses a smaller font size than the last. It's easy to get to the point where the last level can't be read. I'd advise limiting your bulleted lists to three levels at most and ideally just two levels to avoid this issue.

(A good template will limit this. So, for example, the Ion Boardroom theme stops decreasing font size when the font size reaches 12 point.)

* * *

If you need to cut, copy, or paste text from within a slide, it works much the same way as it did for the slides in the left-hand pane.

To cut text, highlight the text you want to cut and then use Ctrl + X or go to the Clipboard section of the Home tab and choose Cut from there. You can also right-click and choose Cut from the dropdown menu.

As you'll recall, cutting text removes it from its current location but still allows you to paste that text elsewhere.

To copy text, highlight the text you want to copy and then use Ctrl + C or to go to the Clipboard section of the Home tab and choose Copy from there. You can also right-click and choose Copy from the dropdown menu.

Copying keeps the text in its current location but also allows you to paste that text elsewhere.

To paste text, click on the location where you want to place the text you copied or cut and then use Ctrl + V. If you paste text this way it will take on the formatting of the location where you paste it. Your other options are to click where you want to paste the text and then go to the Clipboard section of the Home tab and click on the arrow under Paste or right-click.

This will give you the Paste Options list of choices:

The option with the lower case a in the bottom right corner will use the formatting of the location where you are pasting your text.

The option with the paintbrush in the bottom right corner will keep the formatting the text already had.

The option with the small picture in the bottom right corner will paste the selected text in as an image. (You will not be able to edit this text after it's pasted because it will no longer be considered text.)

The option with the large A in the bottom right corner, will paste as text only. (This should generally have the same result as pasting with the destination theme, the first option.)

(There are more specialized paste options available under the Clipboard option, but for a beginner level I don't think they're worth discussing here. If you want to look at them click on Paste Special from the dropdown.)

* * *

If you need to remove text you can either cut that text or you can use the Delete or Backspace keys. Backspace will delete text to the left of the cursor. Delete will delete text to the right of the cursor.

If you've highlighted the text you want to delete then either one will work.

Delete and Backspace can also delete bullet points or the numbers or letters in a numbered list.

FORMATTING TEXT IN A PRESENTATION

All of the templates include text that's of a pre-defined size and using a pre-selected font. If you can stick to the defaults, your life will be much easier because then you can simply add a new slide and everything will be all set to work together.

But it's quite possible that at some point in time you'll want to customize a font size or change the font used or maybe even the color of the font. So in this section we'll walk through how to do that. Just know that doing so will add complications to your life.

As soon as you type text into a presentation slide you should see that the Font section of the Home tab is not only visible but populated with values. (Before you add text it will be visible but grayed out.)

Let's walk through what you can do using these options. For each option, you need to have selected the text you want to edit before you make your choice.

Font

The top left option in the Font section is where you select the font for your presentation. The current font will be visible in the dropdown box.

If you want to change that font you can click on the dropdown arrow and choose from the list of available fonts. The list will show the theme fonts first, your recently used fonts next, and then all available fonts in alphabetical order.

If you start typing a font name that will take you to that portion of the alphabetical listing. So typing T in the white space shows Tahoma and takes me to the T section of the font listing.

For a font that's later in the alphabet, it's often easier to start typing the name, but there is a scroll bar on the right-hand side of the listing that you can use to move through your selections.

The name of the fonts are written in that font to give you an idea of what each font will look like when used.

Another option is to right-click on your text to bring up what I call the mini-formatting bar. It has a font dropdown menu just like the one on the Home tab that you can use to change the font.

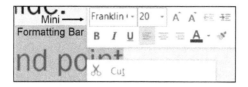

Or you can right-click on your text, choose Font from the dropdown menu, and then change the Latin Text Font box in the Font dialogue box to the font you want using the dropdown to select your font and then clicking on OK.

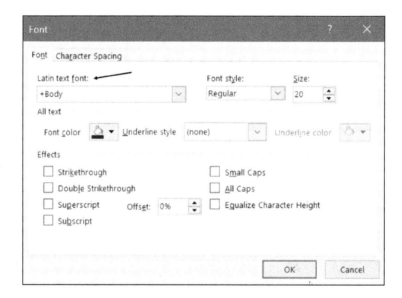

Font Size

The next option in the Font section of the Home tab is your font size. This determines how big the text is on the slide. 36 point is a good visible size for headers. 24 or 18 point is a good size for your main body text but you could probably go as small as 12 point. If you're doing handouts instead of a presentation, you can use 8 or 10 point for footnotes. Don't go smaller than that.

You have a number of options for changing your font size.

The first is to click into the box with the current font size and type a new value.

You can also click on the dropdown arrow next to the current font size and choose from one of the values in the dropdown.

Or you can use the Increase Font Size and Decrease Font Size options that are next to the font size dropdown menu and look like the letter A with either an up or a down arrow in the top right corner. If you use the increase and decrease font size options, the only values available to you are the ones in the dropdown menu.

You can also right-click and use the mini-formatting toolbar or right-click and choose Font from the dropdown menu and then change the font size in the Font dialogue box.

There are also control shortcuts for changing the font size upward or downward one level, but I honestly don't recommend learning them because I don't think you'll need them often enough to make it worthwhile. They are Ctrl + Shift + > to increase one font size and Ctrl + Shift + < to decrease one font size.

Font Color

The option in the bottom right corner of the Font section that looks like an A with a red line under it (at least when you first open PowerPoint—the line color can change as you work in PowerPoint) is where you can change the color of your text.

Click on the dropdown arrow and you'll see seventy different colors you can choose from.

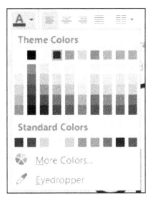

If you need a different or a custom color, click on More Colors. This will bring up the Colors dialogue box. On the Standard tab you can choose from the honeycomb of colors available by clicking on any of the colored squares. On the Custom tab you can input your own RGB values or HSL values. You can also click into the rainbow of colors above that or move the slider for different shades of a color. The color you've selected will show under New in the bottom right corner of the Colors dialogue box.

Another option available to you in PowerPoint is the eyedropper. When you click on the dropdown arrow for Font Color the bottom option in that list is the Eyedropper Text Fill. If you click on this and then click on a color in one of your presentation slides, PowerPoint will grab that color you clicked on. It will then be shown as a color you can use under Recent Colors in the color dropdown menu.

(I use the eyedropper often to pull a color from one of my book covers when I'm creating a related presentation. I import the cover, pull the color from it using the eyedropper, and then delete the cover.)

All of these color options are also available by right-clicking to pull up the mini-formatting bar.

You can also right-click, go to Font in the dropdown menu, and then on the Font tab of the Font dialogue box choose a font color from there. (The Font dialogue box dropdown does not, however, include the eyedropper option.)

Bolding Text

To bold text, highlight your text and click on the capital B on the left-hand side of the second row in the Font section of the Home tab.

You can also right-click on your selected text and click on the capital B in the mini-formatting bar.

Or you can use Ctrl + B after you've selected your text.

Or can right-click, choose Font from the dropdown menu, and then change the Font Style in the Font dialogue box to Bold. Or Bold Italic if you want both bold and italic.

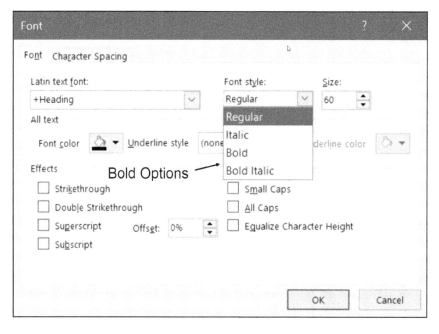

To remove bolding from text, select the text and either click on the capital B or use Ctrl + B once more. If you select text that is partially bolded and partially not bolded, you will need to do this twice because the first time will apply bolding to the entire selection and the second time will remove it from the entire selection.

You can also select your text, right-click, choose Font from the dropdown menu, and then change the Font Style to Regular.

Italicizing Text

To italicize text, select your text and click on the slanted I on the left-hand side of the second row in the Font section.

You can also click on the slanted I in the mini-formatting bar.

Or you can use Ctrl + I.

Or you can right-click, choose Font from the dropdown menu, and then change the Font Style in the Font dialogue box to Italic. (Or Bold Italic if you want both bold and italic.)

To remove italics from text, select the text and either click on the slanted I or use Ctrl + I once more. If you select text that is partially italicized and partially not, you will need to do this twice because the first time will apply italics to the entire selection and the second time will remove it from the entire selection.

You can also just right-click, choose Font from the dropdown menu, and then change the Font Style in the Font dialogue box to Regular.

Underlining Text

To underline text, click on the capital U with a line under it on the left-hand side of the second row in the Font section.

You can also click on the capital U with a line under it in the mini-formatting bar.

Or you can use Ctrl + U.

Or you can right-click, select Font from the dropdown menu, go to the Font dialogue box and choose from the dropdown menu next to Underline Style.

To remove underlining from text, select the text and either click on the capital U with a line under it or use Ctrl + U once more. If you select text that is partially underlined and partially not, you will need to do this twice because the first time will apply underlining to the entire selection and the second time will remove it from the entire selection.

You can also go to the Font dialogue box and change the Underline Style to (none).

If you want a different underline style than just the basic single line underline, it's best to use the Font dialogue box. (So right-click and choose Font from the dropdown menu and then change the Underline Style.) There you'll have the choice of a double-line or a bolder line than standard as well as dotted lines and wavy lines in various styles. (Don't get carried away here. Remember, clean and simple is better than fancy and complicated when trying to convey information to other people.)

To remove a non-standard underline, select the text and use Ctrl + U or click on the U in the Font section until there is no underline remaining. It will usually take two tries, because the first time will convert it to a standard underline. You can also just go back to the Font dialogue box and change the underline style back to none.

Change Case

If you want your text to be in all caps or if you have text that is already in all caps that you want to have in normal case, then you will need to change the case of that text.

You can do this in the Font section of the Home tab by clicking on the arrow next to the Aa in the bottom row on the right-hand side. This will give you a dropdown menu with choices for sentence case, lower case, upper case, capitalize each word, and toggle case.

Sentence case will capitalize the first letter of the first word in each sentence or text string.

Lower case will put all of the letters in lower case.

Upper case will put all of the letters in upper case.

Capitalize each word will capitalize the first letter of each word.

Toggle case will put the first letter of each word in lower case and all other letters in upper case.

Clear Text Formatting

If you've edited a text selection and want to return it to the default for that theme, you can select the text and then click on the small A with an eraser in the top right corner of the Font section. (If you hold your mouse over it, it will show as Clear All Formatting.)

This will change the selection to whatever font, font size, and font formatting would be appropriate for that location within that theme. It does not change the case of the letters but it will revert the font, font color, font size, and any bold, italics or underline back to the default for the theme.

Other

You'll note that there were a few other options available in the Font section of the Home tab (text shadowing, strikethrough, and character spacing) as well as additional options in the Font dialogue box.

I've chosen not to cover them here because I want to keep this guide focused on a basic level of PowerPoint presentation and those are ones I expect you wouldn't use often, but if there's a text effect you want to apply in a PowerPoint slide that I didn't cover, the Font section of the Home tab or right-clicking and choosing Font to bring up the Font dialogue box are a good place to start.

For more advanced text formatting you'll want to look to the Format tab under Drawing Tools that will appear when you click on any text in your presentation. That's intermediate level so we're not going to cover it here.

Next let's talk about paragraph-level formatting.

FORMATTING PARAGRAPHS
IN A PRESENTATION

What we just talked about are formatting changes that you can make at the word level. But there are other changes you can make at the paragraph level. These are generally covered in the Paragraph section of the Home tab but some of them are also available in the mini formatting bar or by right-clicking and choosing Paragraph from the dropdown menu.

With the paragraph formatting options you don't have to highlight all of the text, you just need to be clicked onto the line or into the section you want to change. Let's start with one we already covered earlier, Decrease List Level and Increase List Level.

Decrease List Level/Increase List Level

A lot of PowerPoint presentations rely on using bulleted lists. And when you use a bulleted list you will often want to either indent the next line or decrease the indent of the next line.

To indent the next line, you can either click at the beginning of the line and use the Tab key. Or you can click anywhere on the line and use the Increase List Level option in the Paragraph section of the Home tab.

This is the one with a right-pointing arrow embedded in a series of lines that is on the top row and towards the middle on the left-hand side.

To decrease the indent on the next line, you can either click at the beginning of the line and use Shift + Tab (so hold down the Shift key and then the Tab key) or you can click anywhere on the line and use the Decease List Level option in the Paragraph section of the Home tab. This is the one with a left-pointing arrow embedded in a series of lines that is on the top row and also towards the middle on the left-hand side.

If the decrease list level option is grayed out (like it is in the picture above) that's because you're already at the far left-hand side and can't decrease the indent any further.

These options may or may not be available with plain text that isn't already bulleted or numbered. It will depend on where the text is located within the presentation slide.

Left-Align/Center/Right-Align a Paragraph

Your next option is to change the alignment of the text in your paragraph.

You have four options. You can have left-aligned text, meaning that each new line starts along the left-hand side of the text box. You can have centered text, meaning each line is centered within the text box. You can have right-aligned text, meaning each line ends along the right-hand side of the text box. Or you can have justified text meaning your text will be spread out across the text box so that it's even on both the right-hand edge and the left-hand edge.

All of this occurs within a single text box. If you look closely at the slide formats you'll see that each section with a "Click to add text" or similar message is within a box with a dotted line border. This is a text box. So any changes you make to your text to align it will be made not with respect to the entire PowerPoint slide but instead with respect to the boundaries of that specific text box.

Here are examples of all four options using a text box that has the same dimensions.

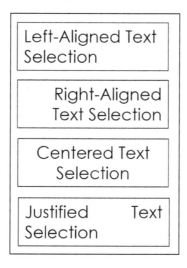

Depending on where your text is and what type it is, your selection will either apply to just the line of text you're clicked onto or all of the contents of the text box. So you may have to do some fiddling around to get the text aligned the way you want it. If you highlight rows of text and then make your alignment choice, all of the rows will change at once.

You can also right-click, choose Paragraph from the dropdown menu, and then choose your alignment option from Alignment dropdown menu in the General section of the Paragraph dialogue box. That also gives you the option to have distributed text.

Top/Middle/Bottom Align Text

You can also align text within a text box along the top, middle, or bottom of that text box. To choose which alignment option you want, go to the Paragraph section of the Home tab and click on the arrow next to Align Text in the middle on the right-hand side of the section.

Choose the option you want from the dropdown menu. Top-aligned text will have the first row at the top of the text box. Bottom-aligned text will have the last row at the bottom of the text box. Middle-aligned text will have the rows of text centered between the top and bottom of the text box

Your choice will apply to all text within the text box.

Using Multiple Columns

If you want your text displayed on a slide in multiple columns you have two choices. First, you can choose a slide layout that has two equally sized sections like the Two Content slide format and then input your text into both of those boxes, split evenly across the two boxes.

Or you can use the multiple column formatting option. To split a column into multiple columns, simply click anywhere within that column and then go to the Paragraph section of the Home tab and click on the arrow next to the Add or Remove Columns option. (This is the one in the center of the bottom row of that section that shows two sets of lines side by side with a dropdown arrow on the right-hand side.)

You can choose between One Column, Two Columns, Three Columns, or More Columns.

To split a list of values into two columns, select Two Columns. To change a list that is in multiple columns back to a single column, choose One Column.

When you click on More Columns you can specify not only the number of columns, but the spacing between them.

The way multiple columns work is that PowerPoint will fill the first column completely before it moves on to putting text into the second column. This means you may have to use extra enters to get half of your list into the second column. Otherwise you may end up with a column with ten entries next to a column with two entries. Better to go to the seventh line in that list and enter until six of your entries are in the first column and six are in the second column.

(If that sounded confusing, just try it in PowerPoint and it'll make more sense.)

Change Spacing Between Lines of Text

If you want to change the amount of space that appears between lines of text, you can do so by going to the Paragraph section of the Home tab and clicking on the arrow next to the Line Spacing option. This is the one with up and down arrows on the left-hand side of a group of lines that is located in the center of the top row.

Click on the arrow to see the available options, but be careful because it applies that space to any lines you have, even ones you might want to keep together.

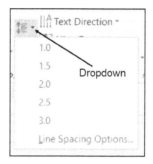

Your other, and perhaps better, option is to right-click and choose Paragraph from the dropdown menu. This will bring up the Paragraph dialogue box. In the Spacing section you can specify the size of the space before and after each paragraph. This can be a way of putting space between bullet points or paragraphs while keeping the lines within a bullet point or paragraph close together.

Bullets and Numbering

By default, most of the templates include bullets within the main body of each presentation slide. If you want to change the type of bullet, turn off bullets for a specific line, add a bullet to a specific line, or change the bullets to numbers, then you can do so with the Bullets and Numbering options in the top left corner of the Paragraph section of the Home tab.

To change the type of bullet, click on the row you want to change or highlight all of your rows if there's more than one, and then go to the Bullets option (the one with dots next to lines in the top left corner of the Paragraph section of the Home tab) and click on the dropdown arrow.

You'll see a box around the type of bullet that's currently being used. Click on None if you don't want a bulleted list. Or click on one of the other options if you want to change the type of bullet. You can hold your cursor over each option to see what it will look like before you make your selection.

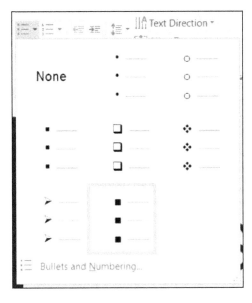

Clicking on Bullets and Numbering at the bottom of that list will let you specify the size of the bullet relative to the text as well as the color of the bullet. (But remember that the more you customize things, the more work you have to do throughout your presentation to keep everything uniform.)

If you want a numbered or lettered list instead (e.g., 1, 2, 3 or A, B, C) then click on the Numbering dropdown. There you can see a list of available numbered list options to choose from.

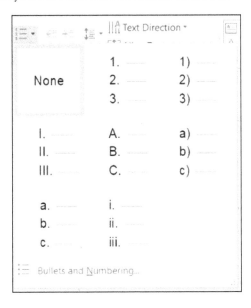

If you need to start at a number other than 1 or a letter other than A, click on Bullets and Numbering at the bottom of the list and then choose your starting point using the Start At box in the bottom right. For lettered lists (A, B, C) you enter a position number and it will change the letter. So a 1 equals A, a 2 equals B, etc. As with the bulleted list, you can also change the relative size of the number or letter compared to the list and change the color of the letter or number.

Another option for changing bullets or numbering is to right-click and go to either Bullets or Numbering in the dropdown menu.

Format Painter

If you ever find yourself in a situation where the formatting on one section of your presentation or your slide doesn't match another and you just want to take the formatting from one of the two and transfer it to the other, then the Format Painter is the easiest way to do so. It's located in the Clipboard section of the Home tab and looks like a little hand broom to me. (Given the name it's obviously a paintbrush.)

To use it, first highlight the text that's formatted the way you want. Next, click on the Format Painter. Then highlight the text that you want to be formatted that way. The formatting should transfer over, including font, font size, font color, line spacing, and type of bulleting/numbering.

Do not click anywhere else in between those steps and do not try to use the arrows to move between sections of text. Highlight, click, highlight. (Otherwise you might carry the formatting to the wrong text.)

This tool can be a lifesaver if someone has done weird things in a presentation you're trying to fix.

If the result isn't what you wanted or expected, then use Ctrl + Z to undo it and try again. Sometimes with paragraphs of text it can matter whether you selected the initial paragraph from the beginning or from the end. So if the formatting didn't transfer the way you thought it should, try selecting from the bottom of the paragraph up instead.

If you have more than one place you want to transfer formatting to, you can double-click on the Format Painter tool and then click on all of the text you want to change. It will stay selected until you click on it once more or hit Esc.

Other

As with formatting text you'll notice that there were a couple paragraph formatting options I didn't cover here. (SmartArt and Text Direction). If you do find yourself wanting to use either option they're available in the Paragraph section of the Home tab, but they shouldn't be needed for a basic presentation.

ADDING A TABLE TO A
PRESENTATION SLIDE

Now that we've covered how to add text to your presentation and then format it, let's discuss how to add a table of data or a picture to your presentation.

If you look at a blank content slide that hasn't had any text added to it yet, you'll see in the center of the text box for most of these slides that there's a series of images. This is from a text box in a Two Content slide:

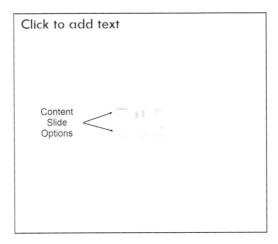

These are options you have other than just typing text into that box. Your options are Insert Table, Insert Chart, Insert a SmartArt Graphic, Pictures, Online Pictures, and Insert Video.

Once you choose one of these options you can't then type in that area. It's one or the other. (Although you could add a text box to the slide and put in text that way if you wanted. That's intermediate-level so we're not going to cover it here but the option can be found on the Insert tab in the Text section.)

We're not going to cover all of the non-text options in this guide, just adding a table and inserting a picture.

Let's start with the table option.

Insert Your Table

The first option in that set of images is to Insert Table.

Click on it and you'll see the Insert Table dialogue box. It lets you specify the number of columns and rows you want in your inserted table.

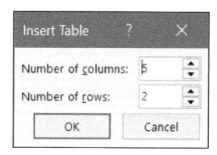

After you've chosen how many columns and rows you want, PowerPoint will insert a blank table with that number of columns and rows into that text box in your presentation. The first row will be formatted as a header row (so in a different color).

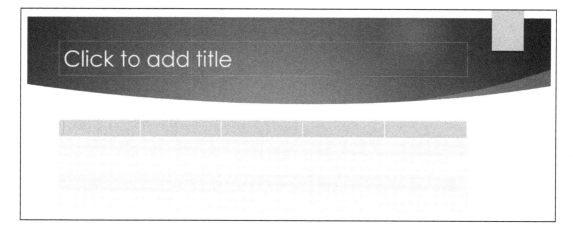

You can then click into any cell in that table to add your information. The colors used to create the table will match the theme you're using.

(If you look at each theme you'll see a set of colored squares at the bottom of the image for that theme. Those are the colors that are used for text, bullets, tables, and SmartArt for that theme. You can change that if you want under the Design tab under Table Tools, but the purpose of a theme is to use a coherent color scheme that all works together.)

Adding Text or Numbers to Your Table

To add text or numbers to your table, just go to the cell in the table where you want to add your text and start typing. If you enter text that is wider than the width of the column, it will automatically go to the next line and the row height will change to make sure all of the text is visible.

If you have the information in an existing table in Word or Excel, you can copy the information from that table into PowerPoint by highlighting the cells in Word or Excel, using copy (Ctrl + C), and then clicking into the first cell in the PowerPoint table where you want to place that information and using paste (Ctrl + V).

(This is sometimes the easier option when you have a lot of number formatting to do.)

Aligning Text Within Cells

If after you've entered text into your table you want to change the alignment of the text so that it's centered or left-aligned, etc. you can do this by highlighting the cells you want to change, going to the Layout tab under Table Tools, and going to the Alignment section. The top row where you see the three options with lines is where you can choose to left-align, center, or right-align text. The second row where you see the three boxes with lines in them is where you can choose to place text at the top, center, or bottom of each cell.

Adding Additional Rows or Columns

If you add a table and then want additional rows added to the table, simply use the tab key from the last cell in the last row of the table and PowerPoint will add a new line.

You can also highlight a row, go to the Layout tab under Table Tools, and choose Insert Above or Insert Below from the Rows & Columns section to add a row.

To add a column, highlight an existing column, go to the Layout tab under Table Tools, and choose Insert Left or Insert Right from the Rows & Columns section.

You can also highlight a row or column and right-click to bring up the mini formatting bar which has an Insert option with a dropdown arrow for inserting rows and columns.

Deleting a Row or Column

To delete a row or column from a table that you've decided you don't want, you can highlight the row or column, right-click and choose Cut or use the Delete option on the mini formatting bar.

Or you can click into a cell in that row or column, go to the Layout section of Table Tools, and under the Rows & Columns section click on the dropdown arrow under Delete. From there you can choose Delete Columns, Delete Rows, or Delete Table.

Deleting the Table

To delete the entire table, right-click and use the Delete option in the mini formatting bar to choose Delete Table. Or right-click on the table and choose Select Table from the dropdown and then use the Delete or Backspace key.

Or hold your mouse over the edge of the table until it looks like a four-sided arrow. Click on the table to select it and then use the Delete key or the Backspace key to delete it.

Moving the Table

Click on the table to select it or right-click and choose Select Table. Hold your mouse over the edge of the table until it looks like a four-sided arrow and then left-click and drag the table to where you want it.

Changing Column Width

To change the width of a column, click on a cell in the column and go to the Layout section of Table Tools and change the value in the Cell Size section for the Width.

You can also hold your mouse over the right-hand side of the column in the table itself until the cursor looks like two parallel lines with arrows pointing off to the sides and then left-click and drag to your desired width or double-left click to get the column to automatically resize to the width of the text that's currently in that column.

When you change the column width under Table Tools it will change just that column's width, so will also change the size of the table. Same with double-clicking to change the column width. If you use the click and drag option, both that column and the one next to it will have their column width changed but the overall size of the table will stay the same. That also means you can only click and drag so far because you'll be limited by the width of the two columns.

Changing Row Height

To change the height of a row, click on a cell in the row and go to the Layout section of Table Tools and change the value in the Cell Size section for the Height.

You can also hold your mouse over the bottom edge of the row in the table itself until the cursor looks like two parallel lines with arrows pointing up and down and then left-click and drag to your desired height. You will be limited in how skinny you can make a row based upon the font size for the text in the table.

With both methods, just that row's height will change so the table height will change as well.

Resizing the Table

To change the dimensions of an entire table, you can click on the table and then left-click and drag from any of the white squares around the edge of the table. Be sure that you have a white double-sided arrow when you do so or you may just ended up moving the table around. Clicking on one of the white boxes in the corner will allow you to resize the table proportionately as long as you click and drag at an angle.

You can also click on the table and go to the Layout tab under Table Tools and change the dimensions for the table listed under the Table Size section. If you want to resize the table and have the relative height and width of the table stay the same, click the Lock Aspect Ratio box first. When you do that PowerPoint will adjust both measurements at once to keep the ratio of height to width for the table constant.

Splitting Cells in a Table

You can take one or more cells in a table and split them into multiple cells. To do this, highlight the cell or cells you want to split, go to the Layout tab under Table Tools, and click on Split Cells in the Merge section. This will bring up the Split Cells dialogue box which lets you specify how many columns and rows you want each cell split into. This applies to each cell you selected. So if you select four cells and tell it to split them into two columns and one row, each of those four cells will be split into two columns and one row, so you'll have eight cells where there were four before.

You can also bring up the Split Cells dialogue box by highlighting the cells you want to split, right-clicking, and choosing Split Cells from the dropdown menu.

Merging Cells in a Table

You can also merge cells in a table. In this case, highlight the cells that you want to merge into one cell, go to the Layout tab under Table Tools, go to the Merge section, and choose Merge Cells.

You could also select the cells you want to merge, right-click, and choose Merge Cells from the dropdown menu.

ADDING A PICTURE TO A
PRESENTATION SLIDE

The option directly below Insert Table is Pictures. Click on it and you'll see the Insert Picture dialogue box. By default it will open in your Pictures folder on your computer, but you can navigate from there to any location on your computer where the picture you want is stored. If you click on the All Pictures dropdown option next to the File Name box you can see the picture file types that PowerPoint will accept. (Which looks to be pretty much any type you can image.)

Navigate to where the picture you want is saved, click on the picture, and then choose Insert.

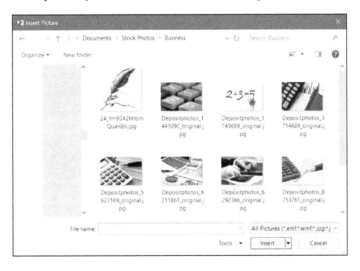

(There is an option there to link instead of insert your photo, but I'd advise against it because it's far too easy to break a link like that. Better to just put the image into your presentation.)

The image will insert into your slide at a size that fits within the text box where you chose to insert it. If the image is smaller than the active area it will insert at its current size, but if it's larger than the active area it will be scaled down and possibly cropped to fit.

(This is for when you use the Pictures icon to insert an image into a text box. You can also go to the Insert tab and choose Pictures from the Images section there to insert a picture on a blank slide.

In that case the image you insert will be centered in the presentation slide and may fit the entire slide if it's large enough.)

Moving a Picture

Once your image has been inserted into your slide, you can click on the image and drag it to the location you want. Left-click anywhere on the image, hold down the left-click, and drag the image to its new location. (It will take the text box it was inserted into with it, but if you then delete the image, the text box will reappear in its original location.)

Resizing a Picture

You can also resize a picture after you insert it into your slide. If you have specific dimensions that you want to use, click on the image and go to the Format tab under Picture Tools. On the far right-hand side you'll see the Size section.

Change either the height or the width and the image will resize proportionately. (So PowerPoint will adjust the other measurement to keep the height to width ratio the same.)

You can also click onto the image and then left-click on any of the white boxes around the perimeter and drag until the image is the size you want. This will not resize the image proportionately, so you can easily end up with a distorted image if you do it this way. But if you click on a corner and drag at an angle that usually will work because you are resizing the image on both the horizontal and vertical dimensions at once. (If you don't like the result, remember, Ctrl + Z to undo.)

Rotating a Picture

If you want to rotate the picture that you inserted, click on the image and then click on the little white outline of an arrow circling to the right that's above the image.

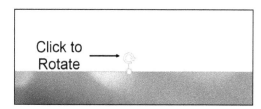

Click and hold this while you move your cursor in the direction you want to rotate the image and it will rotate along with your mouse.

Your other option is to click on the image and then go to the Format tab under Picture Tools and go to the Arrange section and choose Rotate. You can choose from the dropdown menu which lets you rotate 90 degrees right or left or flip the image vertically or horizontally. If you need more options than that, click on More Rotation Options to bring up the Format Picture task pane on the right-hand side of the screen. There you can set your rotation (the third option) to anything you want.

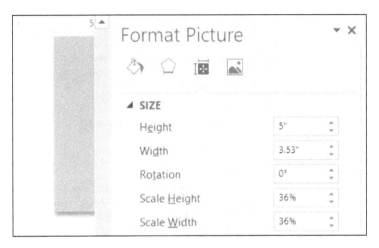

Cropping a Picture

Sometimes I'll drop a picture into a presentation and then realize that I didn't want the entire picture, I just wanted a section of it. (This is especially true when I take screenshots of Excel using Print Screen and then want to just keep a small section of that screenshot for my presentation.) In those cases, I need to crop the image to only show the portion I care about.

To crop an image, right-click on the image and choose Crop from the mini formatting bar. You should then see small black bars on each side of the image and at the corners. Left-click on those bars and drag until only the portion of the image that you want to keep is visible. Be sure when you click and drag that the cursor looks like a bar, because otherwise you might end up resizing the image instead. (If so, Ctrl + Z to undo and try again.)

When you move the boundaries of the image, you'll still see the full image but muted where it's no longer within your new boundaries.

You can click on the image and move it to make sure that the portion of the image you want to keep is within your new boundaries. (And if you insert an image that PowerPoint cropped and you want a different portion of that image to be visible, you can choose to "crop" the image and then click and drag until the portion of the image you wanted to be visible is, without actually changing the boundaries of the image.)

When you're satisfied that the cropped portion is what you want, hit Esc. You should now have just the cropped portion of the image.

Your other option for cropping is to go to the Format tab under Picture Tools and choose Crop from the Size section. The first option in the dropdown is a simple crop. You can also crop to a shape or crop to a specific aspect ratio.

Bring Forward/Send Backward

If you are ever in a situation where you have an image that overlaps a text box, you may need to use the bring forward or send backward options. These options determine which layer is visible when two layers overlap. If you have an image on top that you want in back, you send backward. If you have an image that's hidden that you need to move to the top you bring it forward.

Click on your image, go to the Format tab under Picture Tools, and go to the Arrange section. Choose either Bring Forward or Send Backward depending on what you need to do with the image. If there are multiple layers of images you can click on the arrow instead and choose to Bring to Front or Send to Back to make the image you've clicked the topmost layer or the backmost layer.

Alignment

Another option in the Arrange section of the Format tab is Align. There are a number of options available here. To align an image with respect to the presentation slide, click on the image and then click on the dropdown for Align.

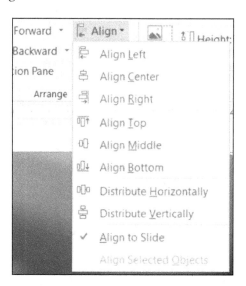

You can choose to align left (place the image along the left-hand side of the slide), align center (place the image in the center of the slide as judged from left to right), align right (place the image along the right-hand side of the slide), align top (place the image along the top edge of the slide), align middle (place the image in the center of the slide as judged from top to bottom), or align bottom (place the image along the bottom edge of the slide).

Distribute horizontally will center the image judged from left to right. Distribute vertically will center the image judged from top to bottom. Where this one matters is when you have multiple images selected at once. If you have multiple images selected at once then it will take those images and distribute them either across the width of the slide (horizontally) or from top to bottom (vertically) so that there is equal space between the images and the edges of the slide.

If you do have multiple images, you can select those images, and then under Align choose Align Selected Objects and instead of aligning the objects to the presentation slide it will align them to one another. So, for example, align right would move the left-hand object into alignment with the right-hand object.

Picture Styles

There is a Picture Styles section in the Format tab under Picture Tools. Click on your image to see what choices are available to you and then click on each style to see what it will look like in your slide. What these generally do is add borders or shading to your picture.

(I would recommend not using these unless you have a good reason to do so. I can't tell you how many times I've seen a presentation that had all sorts of added weirdness that distracted from what the presenter was trying to say. I'm a firm believer in keeping it simple.)

Adjusting a Picture

In the same way that I don't think you should use Picture Styles unless you need to, I'm going to advise against getting too fancy with adjusting a picture you import into your presentation, but I will point out the existence of the options for you. If you go to the Format tab under Picture Tools you'll see on the far left-hand side that there is a section called Adjust.

Click on the arrow under Corrections and you can see a series of options for sharpening or softening an image and for changing the brightness or contrast of the image. You can see what each option will look like as well.

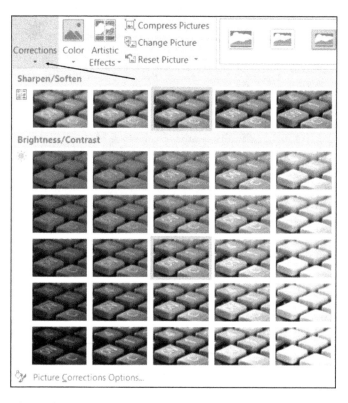

Click on the arrow under Color and you'll see that you can change the color saturation, color tone, or recolor your image.

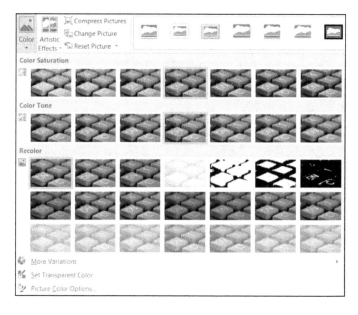

Click on the arrow under Artistic Effects and you'll see that you can apply a number of effects to your image.

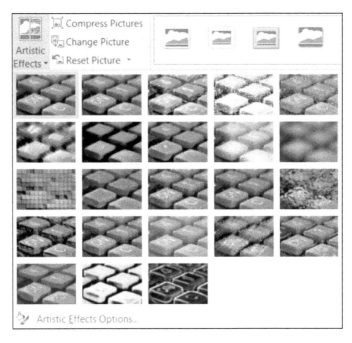

Once more, I wouldn't recommend doing this unless you have a good reason for doing so. Always ask yourself two questions before making a change like this. One, will it still look professional? (And professional means different things in different environments, so what's fine for an advertising agency will not be fine for an investment bank.) And, two, does what I just did make it easier for others to understand my presentation?

If it doesn't look professional, don't do it. And if it doesn't increase other people's ability to understand you, don't do it. The last thing you want is people more focused on what on earth that is than on what you're saying.

ANIMATIONS

If you have a presentation slide with multiple bullet points it's often very useful to have those bullet points appear one at a time. This way people listen to what you're saying instead of trying to read ahead on the slide and see what you're going to say.

The way you get one bullet point to appear on a slide at a time is by using the options under the Animations tab.

First, go to the slide where you want to add animation. Next, click on one of the lines of text and go to the Animations tab. From there click on one of the options in the Animation section.

I recommend using Appear. It simply shows the line without any fancy tricks which can be distracting.

If the slide you're dealing with is just a list of bullet points with no indents and no images, the lines in the slide should now be numbered starting at one and up to however many lines you have.

This is the order in which they're going to appear as you give your presentation. (Usually triggered by hitting Enter, using the down arrow on your keyboard, or left-clicking to advance through the slide as you present.)

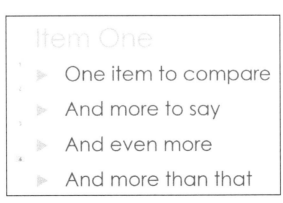

If you have indented lines of text you will probably need to fix their numbering. By default in my version of PowerPoint any indented lines share the numbering of their "parent" line. This is probably best understood visually. See below:

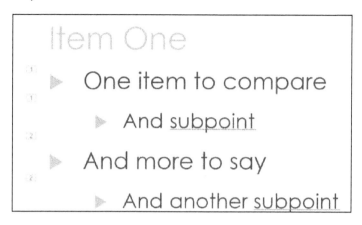

See how we have lines of text with indented lines below them? And how they are all numbered the same? So the first main line of text is 1 and so is its subpoint? And then the next is 2 and so is its subpoint?

That means the main line of text and the subpoint will appear in the presentation at the same time. But usually what I want is to make my main point and then make a subpoint.

To fix this, click into the slide, go to the Animations tab and click on the small arrow in the corner of the Animation section. This will bring up the Appear dialogue box.

Go to the Text Animation tab and change the Group Text option. Depending on how many levels of bullets you have on the slide you will probably need the "By 2nd Level Paragraphs" or the "By 3rd Level Paragraphs" option to get all lines of text to appear individually. Click on OK.

The slide should now show adjusted numbering based upon your choice.

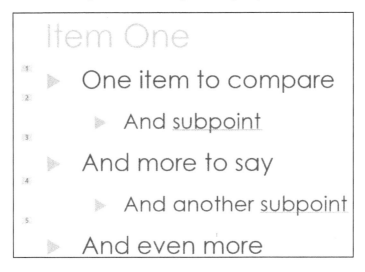

If you also have pictures in your slide, you need to be sure that the pictures are also going to appear or that it's okay that the picture appears first with no text. Also be careful to make sure that the picture appears in the order you want it.

If I have already numbered the lines of text in my slide and I click on a picture and then choose Appear from the Animation section of the Animations tab, it will be numbered last.

The easiest way to change the order in which your different elements appear on the slide is by going to the Animations tab and clicking on Animation Pane. This will bring up a pane on the right-hand side of the presentation slide that says Animation Pane.

It will show all of your elements and the order in which they appear. (You may have to click on the small double arrow under a numbered section to see all of your numbered options from your slide. In the image below I've already done that so clicking on it again would hide them.)

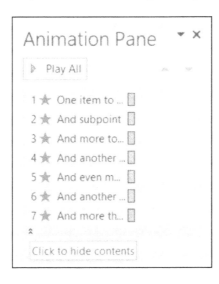

To change the order, click on one of the elements listed and then use the up and down arrows above the list of elements to move that element up or down.

You can also change the level at which your text is grouped in this pane by clicking on the arrow next to one of the text elements and then choosing Effect Options from the dropdown menu to bring up the Appear dialogue box. (Just remember that these choices are applied at the slide level, so any change you make in this manner will apply to all text elements on the slide.)

If you want to have some of your bullet points appear together but others appear separately, the best way I know to do this is to set up the slide as if everything will appear separately and then highlight the rows you want to appear together and click on your option in the Animation section of the Animations tab.

There are other things you can do with animation that we're not going to cover here, such as have each bullet point appear on its own on a timed schedule. But for this beginner guide I just wanted you to know how to structure your slides so that each point you want to make appears separately.

It's tempting to try to make a presentation more interesting with things like this, but if you can't engage your audience with what you're saying then fix what you're saying instead.

I would strongly urge you to keep to just using Appear as your animation option. You can have your bullet points fly in or even bounce in (please, no), but ask yourself if that's appropriate for your audience. If you're presenting to first graders, sure, have a bullet point bounce in. But a potential business client? Eh. Or a group of your professional peers? Uh-uh. Don't do it.

In a minute we'll talk about how to walk through your slides and see your animations in action, but first let's talk about a few general design principles I think are good to keep in mind.

BASIC DESIGN PRINCIPLES

I've touched on this a few times, but I think it's good to take a chapter and discuss some basic design principles to keep in mind as you're preparing your presentation. I'm going to assume here that you're actually intending to use your PowerPoint presentation as a presentation. Meaning, you're going to talk through it and not expect it to talk for you, and that the slides are going to be presented on a projector of some sort to a live audience.

(In other words, I'm not addressing the consulting model of using PowerPoint where you put together a weekly client presentation on a series of slides that you hand out to your client and pack full of information and then walk through even though the client could just read the darned things themselves without paying you thousands of dollars to be there while they do it.)

Font Size

Make sure that all of the text on your slide will be visible to anyone in the room. I'd try to have all of the text be 12 point or larger if you can manage it and with a strong preference for probably 16 point or above.

Font Type

As with all other design elements it can be tempting to use a fancy font. Resist the temptation. You want a basic, clear, easy-to-read font for your presentation elements. This means using something like Arial or Calibri or Times New Roman instead of something like Algerian or Comic Sans.

Summaries Instead of Explanations

The text on your slide should be there as a general outline of what you're going to say, not contain the full text of what you want to say. Think of each bullet point as a prompt that you can look at to trigger your recollection.

The reason you do it this way is because people will try to read whatever you put in front of them. So if you give them a slide full of text they will be busy reading that text rather than listening to what you have to say.

Also, if it's all on the slide, why listen to you at all?

So use the text on your slide as a high-level summary of your next point instead of as an explanation.

For example, I might have a slide titled "The Three Stages of Money Laundering" and then list on that slide three bullet points, "Placement", "Layering", and "Integration". As I show each bullet point I'll discuss what each of those stages is and how it works. If I feel a need to really go into detail then I'll have a separate slide for each one where I provide further information in small bite-sized chunks.

Contrast

You want your text to be visible. Which means you have to think about contrast. If you have a dark background, then use a light-colored text. For example, dark blue background, white text. If you have a light background, use a dark-colored text. For example, white background, black text.

And beware anything that could trip up someone with color-blindness. So no red on green or green on red and no blue on yellow or yellow on blue.

Also, and this may be more of a personal preference, but I try to use the slide templates that have white for the background behind the text portions of my slides. I'm fine with colorful borders and colorful header sections, but where the meat of the presentation is I prefer to have a white background often with black text. (That's the easiest combination to read.)

So I'll choose the Ion Boardroom theme before I'll choose the Ion theme, for example. That one's a perfect example.

Don't Get Cute

PowerPoint has a lot of bells and whistles. You can have lines of text that fly in and slide in and fade away. Or slides that flash in or appear through bars. And some of the templates it provides are downright garish.

Resist the urge to overdo it.

Ask yourself every time you're tempted to add some special effect if adding it will improve the effectiveness of your presentation. And ask yourself what your boss's boss's boss would think of your presentation. I've worked in banking and regulatory environments and I will tell you there is little appreciation in those environments for overly-bright colors and flashy special effects. (Whereas some tech company environment where the CEO wears jeans and t-shirts to work may be all for that kind of thing. Know your audience.)

I do think that using the animation option to have one bullet point appear at a time is a good idea. But you can do that with the Appear option. You don't need Fade, Fly In, Float In, Split, Wipe, etc.

And, yes, it can sometimes feel boring to use the same animation for a hundred slides in a row. But remember the point of your presentation is to convey information to your audience. Anything that doesn't help you do that should go.

ADDING NOTES TO A SLIDE

Now that we've walked through the basics of creating your presentation, let's cover a few other things you might want to do, starting with adding notes to your slides. You can print a notes version of the slides that lets you see each slide as well as your notes. This is a great approach when you have something very specific you want to say but that you don't want to put in the text of the slide.

So how do you add them?

In my version of PowerPoint the Notes portion of the presentation is not visible by default. But at the bottom of the slide I'm viewing there is the word Notes along the bottom border. If I click on this it reduces the size of the main slide and shows me a gray box that says "Click to add notes." If I click into that space and start typing those notes will go on the notes section for that slide.

The other option is to go to the Show section of the View tab and click on Notes. This will also reduce the size of the presentation slide and show the "Click to add notes" section.

Once the Notes section is visible you can click on the same option again to hide it.

OTHER TIPS AND TRICKS

Now that you understand the basics of putting together a PowerPoint presentation, let's discuss a few things you can do in PowerPoint that weren't covered elsewhere but that I think are worth knowing about as a beginning user.

Spellcheck

It's always a good idea to run spellcheck on anything you create for an audience. To check the spelling in your document, go to the Proofing section of the Review tab and click on Spelling. (It's on the far left-hand side.)

PowerPoint will then walk through your entire document flagging spelling errors and repeated words. For each one it will show you its suggested changes on the right-hand side of the screen and will highlight in the presentation slides the word that was flagged as having an error.

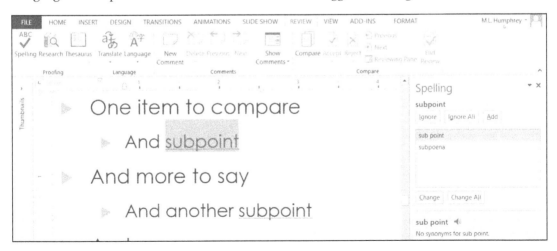

If you don't want to make the suggested change, click on Ignore. If PowerPoint has flagged a word, such as an unusual name, that is used multiple times throughout the document and you want it to ignore all uses of that word, you can choose Ignore All. (You can also choose Add to place it into your dictionary, but be careful with that because it will be added for all documents and that may not be what you want.)

For spelling errors PowerPoint will suggest possible words that you meant. Click on the word in the list that is the correct spelling and choose Change. If you're really bold you could do Change All and all misspellings of that word will be changed throughout the document, just be sure that's what you want.

Find

If you need to find a specific reference in your slides you can use Find to do so. The Find option can be found in the Editing section of the Home tab (on the far right-hand side). Click on Find and the Find dialogue box will appear.

You can also open the Find dialogue box by using Ctrl + F.

Type the word you want into the white text box and then click on Find Next. PowerPoint will walk you through the entire document moving to the next instance of that word each time you click on Find Next.

By clicking the boxes under the search term box, you can choose to just search for whole words only or to just search for words with the same capitalization (match case). This is useful with Find, but essential with Replace.

Replace Text

If you need to replace text within your slides you can use Replace. This essentially pairs the Find option with an option that takes the word you were searching for and replaces it with another. You can either launch the Replace dialogue box by using Ctrl + H or by going to the Editing section of the Home tab and clicking on Replace.

When you do this you'll see the Replace dialogue box. It has a text box for the text you want to find and a text box for what you want to replace that text with.

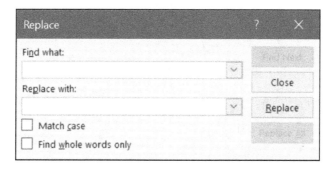

Once you've completed both boxes, click on Replace All to replace all instances of that word in your document. (Replace, when available, will replace only the next usage of the word.) If you don't complete the "replace with" box then you'll be deleting the text you chose to find.

With this one I strongly urge you to use match case and find whole words only. For example, let's say you wanted to replace the name Dan with Bob. Maybe Dan got fired and Bob took his place. (Bear with me, this is just to illustrate a point.) If you don't match case, then PowerPoint will replace every usage of dan with bob. That's probably not going to be a big issue, but if you don't look for whole words only then PowerPoint will take every dan in every word in your presentation and replace it with bob. So, for example, "danger" would become "bobger".

Replacing text is easy to do and easy to mess up. Be very, very careful if you choose to use it.

Replace Font

PowerPoint has a replace function that is unique to it and also incredibly useful. If you go to the Editing section of the Home tab and click on the dropdown arrow next to Replace you'll see that there is an option there to Replace Fonts.

Click on that option to bring up the Replace Font dialogue box.

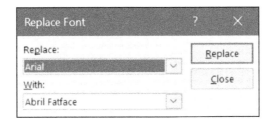

It will show you two dropdown menus.

The first menu is where you select the font that is in your presentation that you want to replace. It should only show the fonts used in your presentation. (Although it also kept showing me Arial whether it was used in the template or not and even after I'd replaced it with another font using the Replace font option.)

The second menu is where you choose the font you want to replace that font with. Once you do this and click on Replace, every usage of the first font will be replaced with the second font. This can come in very handy if you have a corporate requirement to use a specific font that wasn't followed when the presentation was created.

Just be sure to then look back through your presentation and make sure everything looks "right", because different fonts will take up different amounts of space on the page and it's possible that changing over the font could impact the appearance of your slides.

Presentation Size

PowerPoint gives you the choice between two presentation sizes. The standard size is 4:3 and the widescreen size is 16:9. You can also choose a custom slide size.

All of these choices are available in the Customize section of the Design tab on the far right side where it says Slide Size. Click on the dropdown arrow to make your choice.

(If you click on the Custom Slide Size option you can even make a presentation that is in portrait orientation, so like a normal printed report, rather than in landscape orientation. Although, if you're going to do this do it before you start putting together your slides or you'll have a complete mess to fix up. This would not be a good choice for a presentation that's going to be projected on a screen, but could be an interesting idea for a printed presentation.)

PRESENTING YOUR SLIDES

When it comes time to do your presentation, chances are someone will hook up a laptop with your presentation on it to a projector. By default that will show your computer screen. But you don't want someone to see what you've been seeing this whole time as you built your presentation. You just want them to see the slides and nothing else.

So when it comes time to present you need to go into presentation mode in PowerPoint.

To do this, go to the Slide Show tab.

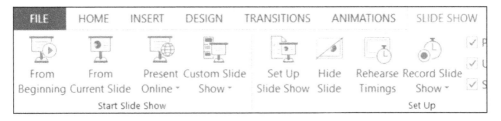

On the left-hand side you have the Start Slide Show section. If you click on From Beginning, this will start a presentation at the first slide in your PowerPoint presentation. If you click on From Current Slide it will start the presentation at the slide that's currently visible.

F5 will also start your presentation from the beginning. And Shift + F5 will start your presentation from your current slide.

Either choice will launch the slides you've created as a full-screen presentation.

The PowerPoint screen you've been working in will still be there and open behind the scenes. You can reach it using Alt + Tab to move through your active windows or you can use Esc to close the presentation version.

To navigate forward through the slides in your presentation, use the down arrow on the keyboard, Enter, or left-click. If you've added animations to your presentation then you'll move forward one animated section at a time. If not you'll move forward one slide at a time.

To move backward, use the up arrow on the keyboard. You can also right-click and choose Previous from the dropdown menu.

Before you enter presentation mode, I'd recommend having any additional windows you're going to want open already so you can easily access them using Alt + Tab.

And it's always a good idea to run through your presentation slides before you present to anyone so you can check and make sure that all the animations, etc. are working. You can do this on your computer screen easily enough by using F5 or the option to view the slideshow from the beginning.

Also—and I hesitate to mention this just because of the potential for things to go wrong and you to not be able to fix them in front of a crowd—there is an option to view your slides in Presenter View. What this is supposed to do is show on your computer screen the slide the audience can currently see as well as your slide notes and the next slide.

But there's a potential to accidentally display that information up on the screen for the audience instead. If that happens, at the top of the screen there is an option at the top of the presenter screen to choose Display Settings and then Swap Presenter View and Slide Show.

If you want to try using Presenter View, right-click on your slide when in presentation mode and choose Show Presenter View from the dropdown menu.

To close a presentation, hit Esc. Or right-click and choose End Show from the dropdown menu.

PRINTING YOUR PRESENTATION

To print your presentation, handouts, or slides with notes, you can type Ctrl + P or go to the File tab and then choose Print on the left-hand side. Both choices will bring you to the same location.

You have a number of print options on the left-hand side and then a preview of what the page will look like when you print it on the right-hand side.

The default is to print all of your slides and in full-page format and that's what your preview will show. But let's walk through everything you can see on this page and your other possible print options.

Print

Right at the top of the page under the Print header is the printer icon. It shows a printer and says Print under it. This is what you click when you're ready to print your document.

Copies

Next to that is where you specify the number of copies to print. By default the number to print is 1, but you can use the arrows on the right-hand side of the text box to increase that number. (Or decrease it if you've already increased it.) You can also just click into the white text box and type the number of copies you need.

Printer

Below those two options is the Printer section. This is where you specify the printer to use. It should be your default printer, but in some corporate environments you'll want to change your printer choice if, for example, you need the color printer.

To do this, click on the arrow on the right-hand side. This will bring up a dropdown menu with all of your printers listed. Click on the one you want. If the one you want isn't listed then use Add Printer to add it.

Printer Properties

If you want to print on both sides of the page you'll need to specify this using Printer Properties which is the blue text visible under the name of the printer. Clicking on that text will bring up a Document Properties dialogue box.

Click on the Layout tab and choose from the dropdown under Print on Both Sides to choose whether to print on both sides of the page and how. If the paper orientation is Portrait, choose Flip on Long Edge. If the paper orientation is Landscape, choose Flip on Short Edge.

You don't need to change the other properties here because they're available on the main screen.

Print All Slides/Print Selection/Print Current Slide/Custom Range

Your next option is what to print. By default, you'll print all the slides in the presentation.

If you were clicked onto a specific slide in the presentation and want to just print it then you can choose Print Current Slide. (When you choose this the print preview should change to show just that one slide.)

If you had selected more than one slide in the presentation and then chose to print, you can choose Print Selection to print those slides.

Your other option is print a custom range. The easiest way to use this one is to type the slide numbers you want into the Slides text box directly below the dropdown. This will automatically change the dropdown selection to Custom Range. Your preview will also change to just show the slides you've listed.

You can list numbers either individually or as ranges. If you list a range you use a dash between the first and last number. So 1-10 would print slides 1 through 10. You can also use commas to separate numbers or ranges. So 1, 2, 5-12 would print slides 1, 2 and 5 through 12.

Full Page Slides/Notes Pages/Outline/Handouts

The next choice is what you want to print.

In the top section you can choose to print full page slides, notes pages, or an outline.

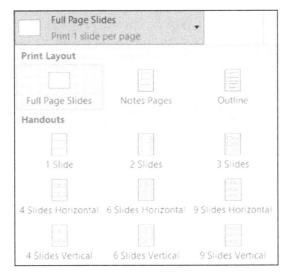

Full page slides will put one slide on each page you print and nothing else.

Notes pages will put one slide per page on the top half of the page and your notes on the bottom half of the page. Each page will be in portrait orientation. (Short edge on the top.)

Outline will take all of the text from your slides and list it out in the same way it's listed on the slides. So if there are bullet points, the outline will have them, too. If there aren't, it won't. Each printed page will contain multiple slides' worth of information. No images are included.

If you want to provide handout slides, you have a number of options to choose from. The one slide option will center each presentation slide in the middle of a page in portrait orientation. (Not recommended.) The two slide option will put two slides on each page in portrait orientation. (This is a good choice for handouts because it's still visible but doesn't waste paper the way the one-slide option does.)

You can put as many as nine slides on the page, but before you do that think about how legible that will be for the end-user. If you have a lot of slides with images it might be fine, but if they have a lot of text on them or if people will need/want to take a lot of notes, no one is going to thank you for putting nine slides on a page.

The horizontal and vertical choices determine whether the slides are ordered across and then down (horizontal) or down and then across (vertical). I think, at least in the U.S., that most people would expect horizontal.

Collated/Uncollated

This only matters if you're printing more than one copy of the presentation. In that case, you need to decide if you want to print one full copy at a time x number of times (collated) or if you want to print x copies of page 1 and then x copies of page 2 and then x copies of page 3 and so on until you've printed all pages of your document (uncollated).

In general, I would recommend collated, which is also the default.

Portrait Orientation/Landscape Orientation

This determines whether what you've chosen to print prints with the long edge of the page at the top or the short end of the page at the top. In general, PowerPoint chooses this for you and does a good job of it. For example, outline should be portrait and full page slides should be landscape.

However, you might want to change this for the handout slides. For one slide, four slide, and nine slide printing, I think landscape is a better choice than portrait. You can judge for yourself by looking at the preview and seeing how large the slides are and how much white space is taken up with each orientation.

Color/Grayscale/Pure Black and White

This option lets you choose whether to print your slides in color or not. The choice you make will probably depend on your available print resources. When you change the option you'll see in the print preview what each one looks like. The grayscale and pure black and white options seem to strip colored backgrounds out of the presentation. The pure black and white one strips color out of the header sections as well.

Edit Header & Footer

At the very bottom of the list you can click on the text Edit Header & Footer to bring up the Header and Footer dialogue box where you can choose to add the date and time, slide number, or a customized footer display to your printed document

Only the Notes and Handouts slides can have a header on them and that's specified on a separate tab.

Once you choose to apply your choices, you can see how it will look in the print preview.

WHERE TO LOOK
FOR OTHER ANSWERS

My goal in this guide was to give you a solid understanding of how PowerPoint works and the tools to create a basic presentation. But there are a number of topics I didn't cover in this guide, such as how to change a presentation slide background color, creating a custom design template, adding timing to your presentation slides, or adding objects or text boxes to a slide.

At some point you'll probably want to learn about one of these things.

So how do you do it? Where do you get these answers?

First, in PowerPoint itself you have a few options. You can hold your cursor over the choices in any of the tabs and you'll usually see a brief explanation of what that choice can do. For example, here is the New Slide option in the Home tab:

You can see that it says this option will let you "add a slide to your presentation." If that brief description isn't enough, a lot of the options have a Tell Me More option below that. Click on that text and the built-in Help function in PowerPoint will open giving a more detailed description of what you can do.

Another option is to go directly to the built-in Help function. You do this by clicking on the question mark in the top right corner of the screen or pressing F1. This will launch PowerPoint Help. From there you can either navigate to what you want or type in a search phrase in the search box.

I often find myself needing more information than this so turn to the internet. If I need to know the mechanics of how something works, the Microsoft website is the best option. For example, if I wanted to understand more about the colors used in each theme in PowerPoint I might search for "colors powerpoint theme microsoft 2013".

It's key that you add the powerpoint, microsoft, and your version year in your search.

When I get my search results, I then look for a search result that goes to support.office.com. There will usually be one in the top three or four search results.

If that doesn't work or I need to know something that isn't about how things work but can I do something, (and this is more true probably in Excel than in PowerPoint), then I will do an internet search to find a blog or user forum where someone else had the same question. Often there are good tutorials out there that you can read or watch to find your answer.

And, of course, you can also just reach out to me at mlhumphreywriter@gmail.com.

I don't check that email daily but I do check it regularly and I'm happy to track down an answer for you or point you in the right direction.

CONCLUSION

So there you have it. We've covered the basics of PowerPoint and at this point in time you should be able to create your own nicely polished basic presentation.

PowerPoint is great for presentations. And it's a valuable skill to have. I've used PowerPoint both in my corporate career as well as my writing career. If you're going to stand in front of a room of fifty (or five hundred) people it's nice to have a presentation up on a screen to help you stay focused on what you meant to say. (And it keeps you from staring down at a podium the whole time while you read your notes.)

It also gives your audience something to look at other than you.

Having said that, you'll have seen in this guide that I have some definite opinions about how PowerPoint presentations can be misused and abused. It can be fun to put a ton of crazy colors and shapes into your presentation and have things bouncing in and zooming out and flashing around, but resist that temptation.

Remember that PowerPoint is a tool, and that its purpose is to help you convey information to your audience. Anything you do in your presentation that takes away from your ability to convey information is a bad thing.

So exercise restraint. (Unless you're in a setting where a lack of restraint will help you, like a presentation to three hundred first graders…In that case, go wild.)

Anyway. Good luck with it. And reach out if you get stuck. I'm happy to help.

Intermediate PowerPoint

POWERPOINT ESSENTIALS BOOK 2

M.L. HUMPHREY

CONTENTS

INTRODUCTION

In *PowerPoint for Beginners* we covered the basics of what you need to know to use PowerPoint if you're using PowerPoint 2013 or an equivalent version of PowerPoint. The discussion covered the basics of navigating and using PowerPoint but relied heavily on using Microsoft's templates rather than trying to create a presentation from scratch. While there was discussion of basic text formatting and how to present your slides, there were a number of areas that weren't covered in that guide.

Probably the most significant of those topics were using shapes, charts, and SmartArt. But there were other topics that weren't covered such using WordArt, equations, and symbols, inserting videos or online photos, using slide transitions, saving presentations as PDFs or images, and inserting headers and footers.

So that's what this guide will cover. It assumes that you already read PowerPoint for Beginners or know the basics of working in PowerPoint and moves on from there.

Alright then. With that said, let's get started.

BASIC TERMINOLOGY

First, let's cover some basic terminology so that you know what I'm referring to when I say certain things. Most of this is the same as what was used in *PowerPoint for Beginners* but without quite as much detail.

Tab

I refer to the menu choices at the top of the screen (File, Home, Insert, Design, Transitions, Animations, Slide Show, Review, and View) as tabs. If you click on one you'll see that the way it's highlighted sort of looks like an old-time filing system.

Click

If I tell you to click on something, that means to use your mouse (or trackpad) to move the arrow on the screen over to a specific location and left-click or right-click on the option. (See the next definition for the difference between left-click and right-click).

If you left-click, this selects the item. If you right-click, this generally creates a dropdown list of options to choose from. If I don't tell you which to do, left- or right-click, then left-click.

Left-click/Right-click

If you look at your mouse or your trackpad, you generally have two flat buttons to press. One is on the left side, one is on the right. If I say left-click that means to press down on the button on the left. If I say right-click that means press down on the button on the right.

Select or Highlight

If I tell you to select text, that means to left-click at the end of the text you want to select, hold that left-click, and move your cursor to the other end of the text you want to select.

Another option is to use the Shift key. Go to one end of the text you want to select. Hold down the shift key and use the arrow keys to move to the other end of the text you want to select. If you arrow up or down, that will select an entire row at a time.

The text you've selected will then be highlighted in gray.

If you need to select text that isn't touching you can do this by selecting your first section of text and then holding down the Ctrl key and selecting your second section of text using your mouse. (You can't arrow to the second section of text or you'll lose your already selected text.)

Dropdown Menu

A dropdown menu provides you a list of choices to select from.

If you right-click on a PowerPoint slide, you will see what I'm going to refer to as a dropdown menu. (Sometimes it will actually drop upward if you're towards the bottom of the document.)

There are also dropdown menus available for some of the options listed under the tabs at the top of the screen. For example, if you go to the Home tab, you'll see small arrows below or next to some of the options, like the Layout option and the Section option in the Slides section. Clicking on those little arrows will give you a dropdown menu with a list of choices to choose from.

Dialogue Box

Dialogue boxes are pop-up boxes that cover specialized settings. For example, when you right-click on a PowerPoint content slide and choose Font, Paragraph, or Hyperlink from the dropdown menu that will open a dialogue box.

Dialogue boxes often allow the most granular level of control over an option.

Panes

Another place where you have a granular level of control over an option is in the formatting panes that are occasionally visible on the right-hand side of your presentation slide. To see one, right-click on a slide and choose Format Shape from the dropdown menu. This will bring up the Format Shape pane to the right of your slide. Since this is a separate section from the main slide, I refer to it as a pane.

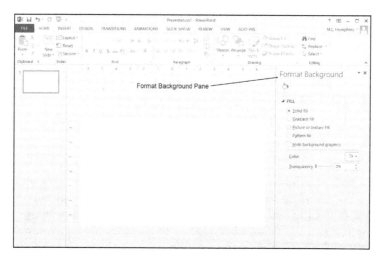

I also refer to the list of slides on the left-hand side in the default view as a pane. So think of pane as just a separate section in your main work area.

Scroll Bar

PowerPoint has multiple scroll bars that are normally visible. One is on the right-hand side of the slides that are displayed in the pane on the left-hand side of your screen (but only when there are enough slides to require scrolling). The other is on the right-hand side of the current slide that you're viewing in the main display section of PowerPoint when there are at least two slides in your presentation.

You can either click in the space above or below the scroll bar to move up or down a small amount or you can left-click on the bar, hold the left-click, and drag the bar up or down to move more quickly. You can also use the arrows at the top and the bottom to move up and down through your document.

In the default view where you can see an entire slide in the main screen, the right-hand scroll bar will move you through your presentation. Clicking on the scroll bar for the left-hand pane will keep you on the current slide but show you other slides in the presentation. (That you can then click on if you want to go to that slide.)

You won't normally see a scroll bar at the bottom of the screen, but it is possible. This would happen if you ever change the zoom level to the point that you're not seeing the entire presentation slide on the screen.

Arrow

If I ever tell you to arrow to the left or right or up or down, that just means use your arrow keys. This will move your cursor to the left one space, to the right one space, up one line, or down one line. If you're at the end of a line and arrow to the right, it will take you to the beginning of the next line. If you're at the beginning of a line and arrow to the left, it will take you to the end of the last line.

Cursor

There are two possible meanings for cursor. One is the one I just used. When you're clicked into a PowerPoint slide, you will see that there is a blinking line. This indicates where you are in the document. If you type text, each letter will appear where the cursor was at the time you typed it. The cursor will move (at least in the U.S. and I'd assume most European versions) to the right as you type. This version of the cursor should be visible at all times unless you have text selected.

The other type of cursor is the one that's tied to the movement of your mouse or trackpad. When you're typing, it will not be visible. But stop typing and move your mouse or trackpad, and you'll see it. If the cursor is positioned over your text, it will look somewhat like a tall skinny capital I. If you move it up to the menu options or off to the sides, it becomes a white arrow. (Except for when you position it over any option under the tabs that can be typed in such as Font Size or Font where it will once again look like a skinny capital I.)

Usually I won't refer to your cursor, I'll just say, "click" or "select" or whatever action you need to take with it, and moving the cursor to that location will be implied.

Slider

Some options in the formatting panes on the right-hand side or in the status bar at the bottom of the PowerPoint main screen use a slider to adjust the setting. This is a horizontal line with a wider bar perpendicular to it. If you left-click on that perpendicular bar and move it to the right or the left it will adjust that particular setting upward or downward accordingly.

ADDITIONAL TEXT AND SLIDE FORMATTING OPTIONS

In *PowerPoint for Beginners* we covered the majority of the text formatting options available in PowerPoint, but there were a few that were skipped. So let's cover those now.

Text Shadowing

Text shadowing is an option that allows you to add a shadow behind your text to make it stand out on the slide. To use this option, highlight the text that you want to shadow and then click on the blurry dollar sign in the bottom row of the Font section of the Home tab. (If you hold your mouse over it it will say Text Shadow.)

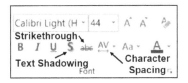

This will automatically add a shadow behind your text like so:

•NON-SHADOWED TEXT
•SHADOWED TEXT

If you want to customize the shadow on your text, right-click on your text, choose Format Text Effects from the dropdown menu, and then go to the Format Shape menu on the right-hand side of the screen and click on the arrow next to Shadow under Text Options.

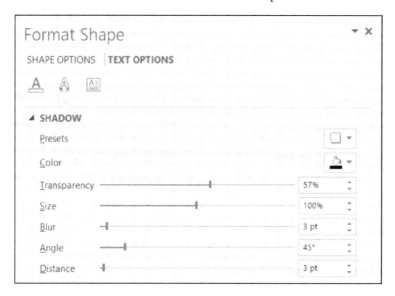

To format just that word that you'd right-clicked on, make the selections you want. To format more than one word, highlight the text you want to change and then make your selections. If you hadn't already added a shadow to the text, you'll need to highlight the text first to apply your shadow using the Format Shape pane.

In the Format Shape pane you can choose from a number of various shadowing options including pre-sets that include inner shadowing, outer shadowing, and perspective shadowing. (Don't worry, each option has a sample image to show what it does.) The pre-sets are the first option in the pane.

If the pre-sets aren't sufficient, you can also specify your own settings by adjusting the color of the shadow, the transparency, the size, the blur, the angle, and the distance. When adjusting these settings remember that Ctrl + Z, Undo, is your friend. Try something, it doesn't work, Ctrl + Z to get back to where you were.

If you need to remove text shadowing, use the pre-set dropdown and choose the option under No Shadow.

Strikethrough

You can also format your text so that it has a strike-through, which is basically a line through the text. This is usually used to show an edit to text where that text was deleted, but you may still need it for text in a slide.

To add a strikethrough to your text, highlight the text, go to the Font section of the Home tab, and choose the option that has an abc with a line through it from the bottom row. (See image above in the text shadowing section. If you hold your mouse over it it will say Strikethrough.)

Another option for adding strikethrough to text is to highlight the text, right-click, choose Font from the dropdown menu, and then choose Strikethrough under the Effects section of the Font dialogue box. This approach also includes a double strikethrough option which will put two lines through the selected text.

Character Spacing

Another option available through the Font section of the Home tab is the ability to change the spacing of your text. So if you want the letters to be closer together or farther apart, this is where you can do that.

To change the character spacing, highlight the text you want to change, go to the Font section of the Home tab, and click on the dropdown arrow next to the AV with a two-sided arrow under it on the bottom row. (See image above in the text shadowing section. If you hold your mouse over it it will say Character Spacing.)

You will then have six options to choose from in the dropdown menu: Very Tight, Tight, Normal, Loose, Very Loose, and More Spacing. You will have the most control over the spacing if you choose the More Spacing option which will bring up the Font dialogue box which allows you to specify the amount to expand or condense the text. But if all you want is a simple option for making the letters closer together or farther apart, the tight and loose options in the dropdown will likely serve your purpose.

Here is an image of the difference between the default options:

Another option for changing the character spacing is to highlight the text, right-click, choose Font from the dropdown menu, and then go to the Character Spacing tab in the Font dialogue box. You can then choose to Expand or Condense the text using the Spacing dropdown menu and then specify by how much in the By pt box. This is the same dialogue box you'll see if you select the More Spacing option in the dropdown menu of the Font section of the Home tab.

Text Direction

In *PowerPoint for Beginners* we discussed how to adjust the text direction within tables, but let's just go over it again here as well, because it can be used on any text in any section of a slide.

By default, at least in the U.S., text will be oriented so that it reads from left to right in a straight line.

You can change this by highlighting your text, going to the Paragraph section of the Home tab, and clicking on the dropdown arrow next to Text Direction. You can then choose Horizontal (which is the default), Rotate All Text 90 degrees, Rotate All Text 270 degrees, or Stacked.

(There is also a More Options choice at the bottom of the dropdown, but it doesn't allow you to choose the actual direction of the text beyond the four main options in the dropdown, so for this specific purpose it really doesn't present anything more than the four main choices do. It's more about where on the page the text will be oriented.)

This is what the four choices look like:

HORIZONTAL
ROTATE 90 DEGREES
ROTATE 270 DEGREES
STACKED

When you change the text direction it will change the text direction for all text within that text box. So if you want some text to be oriented in one direction and other text to be oriented in another direction, like I did above, then you'll need to use multiple text boxes to make that happen. (We'll talk about inserting text boxes in more detail later.)

You can also change the text direction by highlighting your text, right-clicking, choosing Format Text Effects from the dropdown menu, and then clicking on the Textbox option under Text Options (the far right-hand image) in the formatting pane. This will bring up the Text Box options.

The second option is Text Direction which includes a dropdown with the four main choices available through the Home tab. This is the same pane that opens when you choose More Options from the Home tab.

Insert a Hyperlink

To link from text in your presentation to a website or file location, you can insert a hyperlink. To do so, highlight the text that you want to turn into a hyperlink, go to the Links section of the Insert tab, and select Hyperlink. This will bring up the Insert Hyperlink dialogue box which will then give you the option to link to an existing file or web page or another place within your presentation. You can also have the hyperlink create a new document or link to an email address.

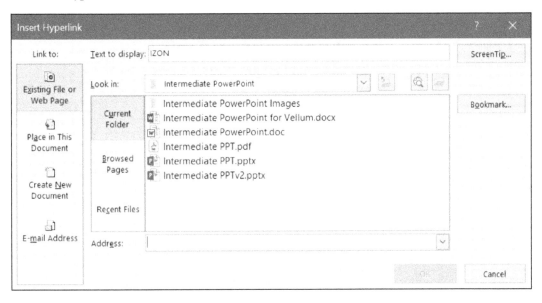

Another option for adding a hyperlink is highlighting your text, right-clicking, and choosing Hyperlink from the dropdown menu. This will also open the Insert Hyperlink dialogue box.

If you want to link to a website address, paste it into the Address field at the bottom of the dialogue box.

If you want to link to an existing file, you can navigate to the desired file using the Look In dropdown menu to choose your location and then selecting from the displayed folders and files directly below that.

To link to a place in the presentation itself, click on Place In This Document on the left-hand side of the dialogue box and then choose the slide you want.

To add an email address click on E-Mail Address on the left-hand side and then paste in the desired email address and provide the subject line you want on the email that this will create.

Insert a Symbol

To insert a symbol, you need to click into a text box on the slide, then go to the Symbols section of the Insert tab, and click on Symbol. This will bring up the Symbol dialogue box which includes a list of recently used symbols as well as a Font dropdown box. With the font dropdown you can choose any symbol listed under that specific font. The Wingdings fonts contain a number of images and symbols such as zodiac signs, checkboxes, clocks, etc.

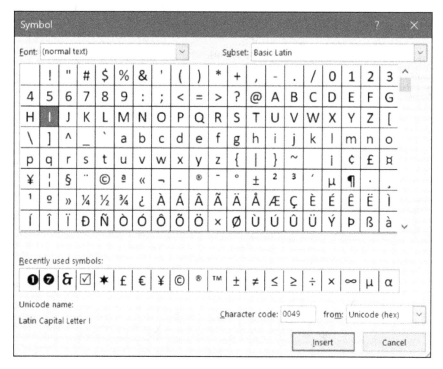

Click on the symbol you want and then click on Insert. The symbol will be inserted into your presentation and you can then close the dialogue box. (You can also type the Character Code in at the bottom of the screen if you already know it.)

Once a symbol has been inserted into your presentation you can change its color, size, etc. using the settings in the Font section of the Home tab or by right-clicking and choosing Font from the dropdown menu.

It appears at least in PowerPoint 2013 that changing the font of an inserted symbol will not change the symbol, but that is something to check for if you're using older versions of PowerPoint.

Use Subscript or Superscript

On occasion you may want to use a subscript (where a portion of the text is lower than the rest) or a superscript (where a portion of the text is higher than the rest). A good example might be a footnote which uses a superscript.

To apply a subscript or superscript to text, highlight that text, right-click, select Font from the dropdown menu, and then choose either subscript or superscript from the Effects section of the Font dialogue box.

For superscript you can also specify how much higher than the surrounding text you want the selection to be and for subscript you can specify how much lower than the surrounding text you want the selection to be as a percentage. Which setting will work best will likely depend on the font size of the text and of your sub- or superscript.

(If you're dealing with equations there is an easier way to do subscripts and superscripts. Look to the chapter on inserting equations for a discussion of that option.)

Format Header Section Background

If you aren't using a PowerPoint template then the slide you're working with will just have a plain white background. In general, I wouldn't recommend this unless you're putting together a presentation that you want to print and trying to save ink because an all-white slide is very generic looking.

One option to make a slide more appealing or less generic is to add a fill color to the header portion of the slide only. To do this, right-click in the text box for the header section and choose Format Shape from the dropdown menu. This will open a Format Shape pane off to the right side that allows you to add a solid fill, gradient fill, picture or texture fill, pattern fill, or slide background fill.

When you click on one of those options you'll then be given more choices to choose from. So if I click on Solid Fill it shows me a color dropdown option as well as a transparency slider.

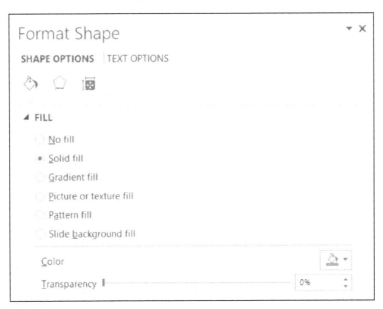

You can choose from any of the seventy basic colors available in the dropdown by clicking on them or you can add a custom color by using the More Colors or Eyedropper options. With the eyedropper option you need that color available somewhere in the presentation so you can "sample" it.

I have pasted in an image of a book cover before and then used the Eyedropper to pull the same color used in that cover when creating related slides. It's a quick and easy way to make sure the colors are consistent between a book and related presentation.

Using Solid Fill will then give you something that looks like this:

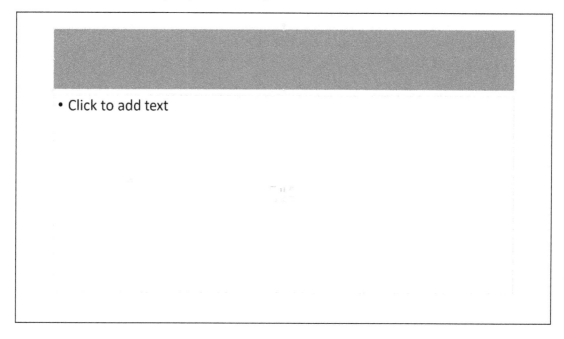

Gradient Fill contains pre-set options for different gradients using six basic colors which you can see in the preset gradients dropdown. If one of those works for you, just click on it.

You can also choose any color you want using the Color dropdown which is available just below the gradient stops settings. From there you can adjust the gradients to match your own preferences using the type, direction, angle, gradient stops, position, transparency, and brightness settings.

The Picture or Texture Fill option comes with a set of 24 textures to choose from. You can also click on the File or Online options to choose a custom picture to use. (Just remember that you need to own the right to use any photo that isn't included within PowerPoint. You can't just pull any image you want off the internet, that's a copyright violation, and if the person who owns the image finds out they can sue you for a lot of money.)

This option also comes with an ability to customize the image offset, scale, alignment, and mirroring type.

Pattern Fill comes with 48 patterns to choose from. The Foreground Color and Background Colors you choose will drive the colors used in the patterns.

Slide background fill is just a quick way to apply the current background on the slide to a text box.

* * *

I will note here that while there are a large number of options for applying patterns and images to your title field, I would be very cautious in using most of them because a lot of them are too busy visually to allow for an effective presentation. They're bells and whistles that may detract from getting your point across. So always stop and ask yourself if your audience will actually be able to read your slide if you use that pattern, image, etc. in the background.

Also, if you are going to use patterns or images, make sure you have a very good eye for design. And keep in mind people who are color blind and can't see the difference between certain colors such as red and green.

Format File Background

In the same way that you can add a background to a text box like the header section of a slide, you can do so to the entire background of a slide.

To do this go to the Customize section of the Design tab and click on Format Background. This will open the Format Background pane. You can also right-click on the outer edge of a slide (outside of a text box) and choose Format Background from the dropdown menu which will also open the Format Background pane.

You can then choose between solid fill, gradient fill, picture or texture fill, and pattern fill just like you did with adding a background to a text box, and it will work in the exact same manner.

I will add the same cautions here as I did above that you need to be careful with a background fill that you don't overwhelm the presentation and make it unreadable. One thing you can do, though, is have text boxes that use a white background on top of a patterned background so that your text remains clearly visible even if the background is more creative.

Here's an example with one of the background patterns:

This is still a very busy image that may take away from someone reading the text you want them to read. If you really want to be that creative, I'd encourage you to explore the provided PowerPoint templates before you try to create your own background and color scheme.

But if you want to do it, that's how. The possibilities are endless.

Next, let's discuss how to easily insert equations into your presentation.

INSERT AN EQUATION

If you're working with mathematical symbols or equations, PowerPoint actually comes with certain common equations that you can just insert into your presentation without worrying about how to find all the appropriate symbols to create them.

To use these equations, go to the Symbols section of the Insert tab, and click on the dropdown arrow under Equation.

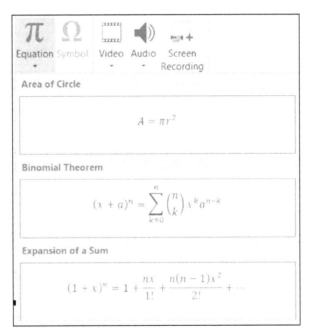

The equations that are available pre-formatted are the area of a circle, the binomial theorem, the expansion of a sum, the Fourier series, the Pythagorean theorem, the quadratic formula, the Taylor expansion, and two trig identities, one involving the sum or subtraction of the sine of two values and one involving the sum of the cosine of two values.

Click on the equation that you want and it will be inserted into your presentation slide as its own text box if you weren't already clicked into a text box, or as an entry in the text box where you had your cursor at the time of insertion.

You can also create your own custom equations. One way to do so is to go to the Symbols section of the Insert tab and under the Equation dropdown choose Insert New Equation from the bottom of the list. The other way is to insert a pre-formatted equation and then adjust it from there.

For a new equation, you'll need to use the Equation Tools Design tab to build your equation from scratch where it says "Type equation here". Click on the symbols or structures you need and then input your specific values into the provided boxes.

The available options for building (or editing) equations are extensive. The Symbols section of the Equation Tools Design tab includes over seventy common symbols and the Structures section includes a wide variety of common notation under the categories of fraction, script, radical, integral, large operator, bracket, function, accent, limit and log, operator, and matrix.

As an example, if I wanted to insert a very simple fraction into my presentation, I could choose to insert a new equation and then go to the Structures section of the Equation Tools Design tab and click on the dropdown under Fraction and then choose the format I want to use. Let's say I want the first option with the numerator and denominator directly aligned. I click on that option and PowerPoint inserts a template of that format into the presentation with two boxes, one for the numerator and one for the denominator. I can then click onto each box and add my values. (I can also click onto each box and add another equation structure or symbols.)

Also, know that under each of the Structures dropdown choices there are common structures that you may need in addition to the preset formulas under Insert Equation. For example, the fraction dropdown has five common fractions, such as delta y over delta x.

For each equation there are three display options available in the Tools section on the left-hand side of the Equation Tools Design tab: professional, linear, and normal.

Here is an example of the area of a circle equation written in each format:

- $A = \pi r^2$
- $A = \pi r^{\wedge}2$
- $A = \pi r^2$

To edit an existing equation, click anywhere within the equation to make the Equation Tools Design tab available.

You can change the size of the text in your equation by selecting the text and then using the Font section of the Home tab like you would with any other text. If the text is formatted as Professional you can't change the font from Cambria Math, but you can still change the font size and bolding, italics, etc.

Also, I was able to change the format of an existing equation from professional to linear or normal, but not to change it back to professional, so keep that in mind before you use that option in the Tools section of the Equation Tools Design tab.

In addition, I had to be careful to click in exactly the right spot in an equation I had created to change a value I'd input in one of those boxes. A few times I ended up deleting the entire section of the equation when I clicked in the wrong spot. Remember, Ctrl + Z, Undo, is your friend.

If you're going to be using mathematical notation in a PowerPoint presentation I highly encourage you to experiment with this option more, but since most users will not need to go in depth on this I'm not going to cover it more than I already have at this point. Just know it's there and probably a lot easier than trying to create a mathematical equation from scratch.

INSERT WORDART

Another option for text in a presentation slide is WordArt. This is another one I'd encourage caution in using because it can be overdone and instead of looking fancy can look garish. What it does is inserts text that has more substance to it than standard text using block letters that then have various enhancements such as a fill color, border color, and/or shading.

You can insert WordArt by going to the Text section of the Insert tab and choosing from the WordArt dropdown menu.

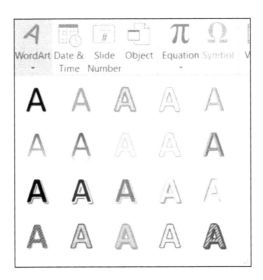

Initially you'll have twenty choices of format to choose from. Click on one of those choices and PowerPoint will insert a text box with that formatting that says "Your text here". You can then replace that text with your own and it will keep the formatting you chose.

Another way to get to the same formatting options is to type text into a slide and right-click on it. You should then see a Drawing Tools Format tab up top in your menu options. This tab allows you to work with the WordArt default styles (under the WordArt Styles section) or create your own (using Text Fill, Text Outline, Text Effects, etc.).

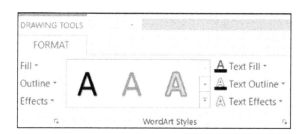

By making selections from the Text Fill, Text Outline, and Text Effects dropdowns in the WordArt Styles section of the Drawing Tools Format tab, you can create a completely customized style for your text.

The Text Fill option allows you to change the surface of the letters to be any solid color, a gradient, or a texture. You can also use a photo for the surface of your text. If you want to use a gradient that is a specific color, so let's say shaded green text, you need to choose the color first and then the gradient.

The Text Outline option allows you to change the color, weight, and style used along the border of each letter. (In other words, it's outline.) To change the color, click on your color choice or choose More Options or use the eyedropper. To change the width of the line that goes around the border, change the weight by using that dropdown menu which will be visible when you hold your mouse over Weight in the main dropdown. Choosing More Options from that list will open the Format Shape Text Options pane and under Text Outline you can then choose a Solid Line or Gradient Line and specify exactly what type of line you want from there.

To change the style of the line that forms the border (solid vs. dashed) you can use the Dashes dropdown menu which is under the Text Outline dropdown menu or you can use the Format Shape Text Options pane. In the Text Options pane dashed lines are under Dash Type under the Gradient Line option.

You can also just go straight to the Format Shape Text Options pane by highlighting your text, right-clicking, choosing Format Shape, and then choosing Text Options in the Format Shape pane.

The Text Effects option allows you to apply a shadow, a reflection, a glow, a bevel, a 3-D rotation, or a transformation to text such as curving your text. Text Effects are either available as a dropdown in the WordArt Styles section of the Drawing Tools Format tab or in the Text Effects section of the Text Options section of the Format Shape pane. (It's the middle option under Text Options whereas Text Fill and Outline are under the first option.)

If you use the curved text effect, you will likely need to adjust the size of the text box to get the text to curve the way you want it to.

In summary, WordArt is fantastic for applications like creating a logo or some other artistic imagery. It should be used with caution for a basic professional presentation. The three main ways to change your text are through the Text Fill, Text Outline, and Text Effect settings either in the

Drawing Tools Format tab or in the Format Shape Text Options pane. You can also use the default WordArt Styles provided in the WordArt Styles section of the Drawing Tools Format tab or in the WordArt dropdown menu in the Text section of the Insert tab.

Now let's talk about shapes.

SHAPES PART 1:
INSERT SHAPES

While we're on the Drawing Tools Format tab, let's talk about inserting shapes into a presentation slide. If you look on the left-hand side of the Drawing Tools Format tab you'll see that there is an Insert Shapes section.

These same options are also available under the Drawing section of the Home tab, and also in the Illustrations section of the Insert tab in the Shapes dropdown menu. So it's really up to you which tab you want to use for inserting either text boxes or various shapes such as arrows.

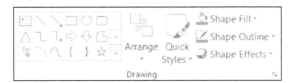

The most common shape I insert is the first one shown, which is a text box. It's the A in the corner of a box with lines in it.

To insert a text box into your presentation slide, click on the text box option and then click onto your presentation slide. The inserted shape will be equivalent to one character. You can then type text and it will expand in size as you type.

To change the size of the text box without adding additional text, click on the box, go to the Size section of the Drawing Tools Format tab and input the height and width that you want. Your other option is to right-click, choose Format Shape from the dropdown menu, go to the Size & Properties section of the Shape Options section in the Format Shape pane, click on the Size arrow to expand that section, and input your desired height and width there.

If you have issues inserting a text box into your presentation slide, try inserting it in an area that doesn't already have a text box in it and then dragging the text box to where you want it to go.

The process for inserting other shapes is basically the same. Click on the shape you want from the menu and then click on a spot in your presentation to insert the shape.

There are some shapes that require multiple clicks to create. For example, Freeform, Curve, and Scribble all require multiple clicks. (You can see a shape's name by holding your mouse over it.)

Freeform will close and complete once you connect your last point to your beginning point.

Scribble requires that you click and hold as you draw your scribble.

Curve will curve your line each time you click on the presentation and will only stop when you use Esc or Enter.

To see the full list of available shapes, click on the downward pointing arrow with a line above it at the bottom right corner of the box showing the shapes in the Home tab or the Drawing Tools Format tab. In the Insert tab, clicking on the dropdown arrow under Shapes will show the full list.

The shapes are then listed by category.

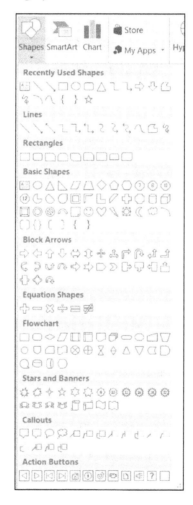

Once more, click on the shape you want and then click into the presentation to insert it.

After you've inserted a shape into your presentation you will probably want to format it. Let's talk about that next.

SHAPES PART 2:
FORMAT INSERTED SHAPES

Once you've inserted a shape into a slide you can then adjust or resize the shape by clicking on it and dragging the white or yellow boxes that are usually located in the corners or on the sides of the content box that contains the shape.

Yellow boxes appear for curved shapes and arrows and are tied to the interior aspects of the shape. They let you change the curve of a curved shape, the width of the base of a two-dimensional arrow, or the placement of the base of an arrow head.

* * *

You can change the direction an arrow is pointing from left to right or right to left by clicking and dragging the base or the tip of the arrow in the other direction. You can also rotate an arrow by clicking and dragging on the white arrow drawn in a circle that is generally visible at the top of the content box for the arrow.

Or you can use the Rotate option in the Arrange section of the Drawing Tools Format tab. There is a dropdown option for Rotate that will let you rotate a shape right ninety degrees, left ninety degrees, flip it vertically, or flip it horizontally.

You can also choose More Rotation Options from that Rotate dropdown to see the Format Shape pane which will let you specify any degree of rotation. (This is also available, of course, by right-clicking on the arrow, choosing Format Shape from the dropdown menu, going to Size & Properties under Shape Options, and then specifying the Rotation value you want in the Size section.)

Note that the degree of rotation is based upon the starting point of the shape. So if you had an arrow that was already pointed off to the right then a rotation of ninety degrees would have that arrow pointing downward since that's ninety degrees from where it started.

* * *

You can change an existing shape to a different one by clicking on it and then going to the Drawing Tools Format tab and choosing Edit Shape from the Insert Shapes section and then choosing Change Shape which will show you all available shapes. Select the one you want.

* * *

In that same Edit Shape dropdown menu you can also choose to Edit Points. This will take the existing shape and show a number of black squares within the shape that you can then click and drag around to change the shape to basically anything you want. Use Esc when you're done. (And remember that Ctrl + Z, Undo is your friend.)

* * *

Once you've inserted a shape into your presentation you can change the fill, outline, and effects for that shape. There are a number of Shape Styles pre-formatted in PowerPoint that you can choose from. Click on your shape and then click on the style in the Shape Styles section of the Drawing Tools Format tab or under the Quick Styles dropdown in the Drawing section of the Home tab.

If you want more control over the appearance of your shape, you can use the Shape Fill, Shape Outline, or Shape Effects options in the Drawing Tools Format tab under the Shape Styles section. They are also available on the Home tab under the Drawing section and in the Format Shape pane under the Fill & Line section of the Shape Options.

The Shape Fill, Shape Outline, and Shape Effect options work the exact same way as the Text Fill, Text Outline, and Text Effects options did with WordArt.

* * *

As mentioned previously with respect to the comment box shape, if you want a shape to be a very precise size you can click on that shape and go to the Size section of the Format Drawing Tools tab and change the height and width shown there. Or you can do so through the Format Shape pane.

* * *

So that's how to format a shape, now let's talk about moving shapes around relative to one another.

SHAPES PART 3:
MOVE SHAPES RELATIVE TO ONE ANOTHER

If you have more than one shape in a presentation slide then you're probably going to end up wanting to move those shapes around relative to one another.

A simple example of this is putting a triangle onto a slide and then adding text onto that triangle using a text box. Depending on which one you added to the slide first, you may need to tell PowerPoint to make the text box the top layer so that it's visible.

This is done using the Arrange options which are available either in the Drawing section of the Home tab or in the Arrange section of the Drawing Tools Format tab. The arrange options include bring forward, bring to front, send backward, send to back, group, regroup, and ungroup.

You can also right-click on a shape to bring it forward or send it back. And you can right-click to group selected shapes (once they've been selected) or ungroup them (if they've already been grouped) or regroup them (if they were just ungrouped).

When dealing with bringing shapes forward or moving them backward, think of the shapes as stacked one on top of the other with the "top" of the stack as the one in the front and most visible. If that shape is overlapping another shape, where the two overlap you will only see the topmost shape. Any portion of the other shape will be hidden.

(For purposes of this discussion I'm considering basically anything you can insert into a PowerPoint slide a shape. So a text box, an image, etc.)

You can use moving shapes forward or backward to adjust which portion of which shape is visible on the slide. For example, a label that needs to be on top of an image should be brought forward so that it is "above" the image.

You can either move a shape one level at a time (with bring forward or send backward) or all the way to the front or back at once (with bring to front or send to back).

In addition to adjusting which shape is "on top", you can also align shapes to one another.

To do this, select the shapes that you want to align, and then choose the type of alignment option you want from either the Arrange section of the Drawing Tools Format tab or the Arrange dropdown in the Drawing section of the Home tab.

The alignment options are align left, center, right, top, middle, or bottom as well as distribute horizontally, distribute vertically, and align to slide.

Whichever alignment choice you make will only include the shapes you selected. The other shapes on the slide will not move. If you choose the option to Align Selected Objects, then the selected objects will align relative to one another. If you choose to Align To Slide instead, then the slide will basically be treated as another shape and your shapes will align to it.

Which direction your shapes move to align will depend on their position relative to one another and the alignment choice you make. So align left will move all shapes to align along the left-most edge of the left-most object. Align right will move all shapes to align along the right-most edge of the right-most object. Align middle will move all selected objects to align along the midline between the left-most edge and the right-most edge of those objects.

Let me walk you through an example.

You have Shape A and Shape B. Shape A is in the top left area of the slide. Shape B is in the bottom right area of the slide.

If you choose to align just the selected objects and align to the top then Shape B will move directly upward until its top edge is in line with the top edge of Shape A.

If you choose to align to the slide and align to the top then both Shape A and Shape B will move directly upward until their top edge is at the top of the slide.

If you choose to align just the selected objects and align to the right then Shape A will move directly to the right until its right-hand edge is aligned with the right-hand edge of Shape B.

If you choose to align to the slide and align to the right then both Shape A and Shape B will move directly to the right until their right-hand edge is aligned with the right-hand edge of the slide.

(I'd recommend just putting two shapes into a slide and playing around with the different options to see how it works. That's really the best way to get a feel for it, but just know that there is logic involved.)

* * *

You can also group shapes by selecting them and then choosing the Group option. Once grouped, shapes are treated as one object and will move together. You can click and drag the whole group or align it to another shape using the alignment options.

You can always ungroup shapes later by choosing the Ungroup option, however, you may need to use Esc to truly ungroup the shapes after making that selection.

* * *

If you have a large number of shapes on a presentation slide, you can also use the Selection Pane which is available in the Arrange section of the Drawing Tools Format tab. Clicking on this option will open a new pane on the right-hand side of the screen that shows every single shape on the slide. You can then select any of the shapes that you want to group or align from that pane rather than trying to select them on the presentation slide itself.

To close this pane just click on the x in the top corner.

SHAPES PART 4:
ACTION BUTTONS

There is a special type of shape that you can insert into a presentation that's called an action button. They're available in the very last section of the shapes dropdown menu.

To see what each one does, hold your mouse over it. For example, the first item in that list is described as "Action Button: Back or Previous".

Unlike the other shapes, when you insert an action button into your presentation this will open a dialogue box where you then need to provide additional information so that the action represented by the shape can be performed.

Here is the Action Settings dialogue box for the back or previous action button:

As you can see, what this one is doing by default is linking to the previous slide. You click on that shape as you're giving you presentation and it will perform the designated action.

There is a dropdown menu available in the Action Settings dialogue box that allows you to choose different actions than just the default. You could set the button to take you pretty much anywhere in your presentation or another presentation or a URL address or even open a file.

The dialogue box that you'll see for each action button is the same one but the default settings will be different depending on the action button you selected.

For example, the sound action button has by default the play sound option checked and an applause sound file selected. (Again there is a dropdown menu provided with numerous sounds to choose from including a custom sound file.)

You can either set an action to occur when you click on it or when you move your mouse over it. Which one occurs will depend on which of the tabs you use in the Action Settings dialogue box. The default is for the action to occur when you click on the action button.

To change the settings for an action button you've already placed in your presentation, right-click on the action button image and choose the hyperlink option from the dropdown menu or click onto the action button and then choose Hyperlink from the Links section of the Insert tab.

Also, the appearance of an action button can be modified the same way any other shape can be modified.

RULERS, GRIDLINES,
AND GUIDES

Okay, now let's talk about a few tools that will assist you in positioning your elements on a presentation slide visually instead of by using the alignment options. Namely, rulers, gridlines, and guidelines.

If you go to the Show section of the View tab you'll see that there are three options listed on the left-hand side: ruler, gridlines, and guides. If the boxes are checked, they're in use, if they're not checked they're not in use.

You can also right-click outside of a content box on any presentation slide to see options for Grid and Guides and Ruler in the dropdown menu.

In my version of PowerPoint I have gridlines turned on by default, so on any slide I'm looking at I can see very subtle dotted lines in the background that intersect to form equally-sized squares across the entire presentation slide except at the edges where the squares are only partial squares. Each complete square is one inch by one inch.

These lines are not visible during a presentation or when the presentation is printed, but when I'm dragging items around on a presentation slide I'm preparing I will often align the items along these gridlines so that I know all of the items are lined up properly.

Guides are lines that run across the slide at any point you specify. They can be either horizontal or vertical. To add one, right-click on your presentation slide, go to Grid and Guides, and then choose Add Vertical Guide or Add Horizontal Guide.

The guide will initially be placed in the exact center of the slide and will be a dotted line that goes off the edge of the slide. To move a guideline, hover your mouse over it until you see two parallel lines with arrows pointing out from them, then left-click and drag. As you drag the line you should see a number. This number indicates how far the line is from the center point. The directional arrow next to the number indicates the direction from the center point. So a right arrow next to a 1.25 means that the guideline is 1.25 inches to the right of the center of the slide.

Guidelines are also not visible during a presentation or on a printed slide. They are just meant to help you place the elements in your presentation.

The Ruler option will add a ruler along the left-hand side and top of the presentation slide. The ruler is numbered from the center point of the slide. So you can see that it will go from say 6.5 to 6.5 with a mid-point of zero.

Rather than adjust the size of a shape in the Drawing Tools Format tab by specifying a value, I will often just click and drag and use the gridlines, guidelines, or ruler to determine where to stop.

HEADERS AND FOOTERS

You can add headers or footers to your slides or handouts fairly easily. For slides it's just a footer, for handouts it's a header and/or a footer.

To do so, go to the Text section of the Insert tab and click on Header & Footer. This will bring up the Header and Footer dialogue box.

There are two tabs available, one for your slide and the other for notes and handouts.

You can add three different items to the footer of a slide: date and time, slide number, and/or custom text.

For date and time, click on the box next to where it says Date and Time. Be very careful here if you choose to update automatically because that may not be what you actually intended. If you make that choice then every single time the document is opened the date and time will change. This is a mistake I often see made with memo fields where people use automatic date and time and then forget they've done so and the date on the memo keeps changing every time someone opens it. The other option is to choose a fixed date and input the date you want.

You can include the slide number at the bottom of a slide by clicking on the checkbox next to Slide Number. In the preview off to the right you can see that the slide number will be placed in the bottom right-hand corner whereas date is in the bottom left-hand corner.

You can also insert customized text in the footer by checking the box next to Footer and then typing in whatever text you want. This text will go in the center section at the bottom of the page.

Oftentimes the footer is used to show a copyright notice. I've also seen it used to note that a presentation was in draft format.

The final checkbox on the tab indicates whether you want the footer included on the title slide. If you actually do have a true title slide, generally you would not want your footer included.

Finally, you can either apply your footer to that specific slide by choosing Apply or to all slides in your deck by choosing Apply To All. Usually you'll want to apply to all.

To add a header or footer to your notes and handouts, click on the Notes and Handouts tab in the dialogue box. You can then add the date and time, a page number, a customized header, or a customized footer to your notes and handouts. This is not the presentation itself, but rather the notes or handouts that can be generated related to the presentation.

Once more, the preview off to the side will show you where each element will appear on the document by showing one of the four boxes on the top and bottom outlined with a darker border. So, for example, if I check the box next to page number then the bottom right-hand corner box will be outlined with a black border in the preview. If I check the box for date and time then the top right-hand corner placeholder will be outlined with the black border.

You can also reach the Header and Footer dialogue box by clicking on either the Date & Time or Slide Number options in the Text section of the Insert tab.

INSERT A CHART:
BASIC STEPS AND CHART TYPES

In *PowerPoint for Beginners* I covered how to insert a table or a picture into a presentation slide, but there were other insert options that I didn't cover because they're more involved. The first of those is the option to insert a chart.

To do this, you can bring up a content-type slide and then click on the second image on the top row which looks like a column chart. If you hold your mouse over the icon it will say Insert Chart.

You can also go to the Illustrations section of the Insert tab and choose Chart.

Whichever you choose, this will bring up the Insert Chart dialogue box.

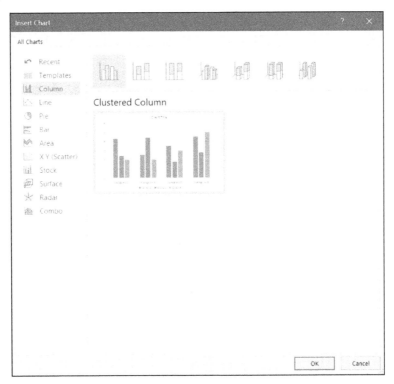

(If you're familiar with Microsoft Excel, you'll notice that this is almost identical to the dialogue box that you see in Excel when you choose to insert a chart.)

To insert your chart, click on the chart type you want, and then click on OK in the bottom right corner. PowerPoint will insert that chart type into your slide and show you a pre-populated data table in a spreadsheet window populated with dummy data. Replace that data with your own and you will have a completed chart.

We'll return to this in more detail in the next chapter, but first we should discuss the different chart types you have to choose from. For those of you who have already read *Intermediate Excel* or *Charts* you can skip the rest of this chapter because it's going to be the same discussion. For those who aren't familiar with the different types of charts, read on.

Note that I am only covering here the most common chart types: column, bar, line, pie, doughnut, and scatter. I am not covering in detail area, stock, surface, radar, or combo charts. They will work on the same principle as the other chart types and I assume you're familiar with them if you're using them.

So.

Column Charts

The first chart option listed is Column Charts. There are seven possible column charts that you can choose from, but I'm going to focus on the first three choices, which are the 2-D versions since most of the 3-D versions are the same except three-dimensional.

For 2-D, you can choose from clustered columns, stacked columns, and 100% stacked columns. Here is an example of all three using the exact same data:

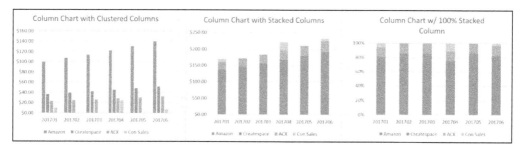

The difference between the clustered columns and the stacked columns is that the clustered columns version puts the results for each variable side-by-side for each time period. You can easily see the height difference between different results, but it can quickly become too busy if you're dealing with a large number of variables. For example, I have nine sales channels I track. Having nine columns side-by-side for each of twelve months would be overwhelming.

In that case, the stacked columns option is a better choice. Like with clustered columns, stacked columns have different column heights for each variable based on their value, but the columns are stacked one atop the other instead of side-by-side for each time period. So you end up with only one column per time period.

The stacked columns option lets you see the overall change from time period to time period based on the total height of the column and for each variable based upon its absolute size as part of the column.

The 100% stacked columns option presents all of the information in one column just like stacked columns does. But instead of basing each section's height on its value, it shows the variable's percentage share of the whole. While you lose any measurement of value (a column chart with values of 2:5:5 will look the exact same as one with values of 20:50:50 or 200:500:500), you can better see changes in percentage share for each variable. (A variable that goes from 10% share to 50% share will be clearly visible.)

As mentioned above, the first three 3-D column chart options are the same as the 2-D options. The only difference is that the bars are three-dimensional instead of two-dimensional. This can sometimes make a chart in a PowerPoint presentation more dynamic, but it can also come off as gimmicky, so use it with caution. My preference is to use charts that keep the focus on the data and not my fancy schmancy presentation skills.

The final 3-D option is a more advanced chart type that creates a three-variable graph. I'm not going to cover that in further detail here since it's more of an advanced topic, but know that it is available for those who want it.

Line Charts

Line charts are the next chart type. There are again seven options listed, but I would recommend only using the first and the fourth options, which are line and line with markers. This is because the other four 2-D options really aren't viable for a line graph. They're meant to do what the stacked columns graphs do and show relative values, but people just don't read line graphs that way. You expect that if there's a line drawn on a graph that it's showing actual values for that particular variable not relative values or cumulative values.

The 3-D option is a more advanced chart type that creates an actual three-variable line graph and we're not going to cover that here. You can use it to create a two-variable line graph with a three-dimensional line, but don't. Keep it simple.

Here are examples of the basic line chart and the line chart with markers:

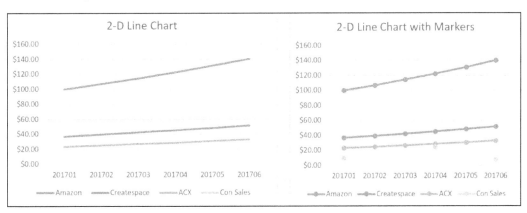

Pie and Doughnut Charts

Next we have pie and doughnut charts under the heading of pie charts.

Pie and doughnut charts are best used when you have one set of variables for one period of time. So, for example, year-to-date values as opposed to values for each month.

There are three two-dimensional pie chart options, one three-dimensional pie chart option, and one doughnut chart option. The three-dimensional pie chart option is the same as the basic pie chart except in three-dimensions. The doughnut chart is basically a hollowed out version of a basic pie chart.

Here are examples of the three two-dimensional pie charts:

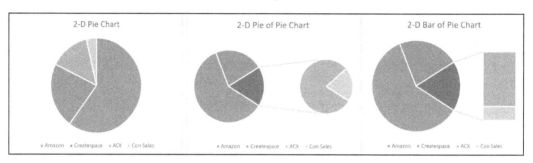

You can choose between a standard pie chart, a pie of pie chart, or a bar of pie chart

If you're only focused on who or what accounts for the biggest share, then you should just use the standard pie chart or the doughnut chart.

If you want to be able to clearly see the results for all of your segments, even the smallest ones, then the pie of pie chart or the bar of pie chart are potentially better choices.

The pie of pie chart creates one main pie chart in which it combines a number of the smaller results to form one segment of the chart. It then breaks out those smaller results into their own pie chart where they each take up their proportion of that smaller part of the pie.

So, for example, in the sample we're seeing here, ACX and Con Sales were combined in the left-hand pie chart but were the only ones in the right-hand pie chart. In the left-hand chart, together they are 18% of the total. In the right-hand chart they are 78% and 22% of that 18%. (If you were to insert labels on this chart, the labels would be the share that each one had of the overall whole, so the smaller pie chart would show 14% and 4% as the labels. It's a bit confusing.)

The bar of pie chart does something similar except it creates a bar chart with the smaller values instead of a smaller pie chart.

In order to avoid confusion, the bar of pie chart is probably the better choice of the two, but honestly I wouldn't use either one if you can avoid it. (The best charts can be read without explanation and I'm not sure that would be true for either of these for your average user.)

Bar Charts

Your next option is a bar chart. Bar charts are just like column charts, except on their side, with a clustered, stacked, and 100% stacked option available in both two-dimensional and three-dimensional versions.

Here are examples of the 2-D versions:

Scatter Charts

The final chart type I'm going to cover here is the X Y or scatter chart (or plot).

Scatter charts plot the value of variable A given a value for variable B. For example, if I were trying to figure out if gravity is a constant, I might plot how long it takes for a ball to reach the ground when I drop it from varying heights. So I'd plot time vs. distance. From that I could eventually see that the results form a pattern which does indicate a constant.

There are five scatter plot options as well as two bubble plot options. We're not going to discuss the bubble plot options here.

The first scatter plot option is the classic scatter plot. It takes variable A and plots it against variable B, creating a standalone data point for each observation. It doesn't care what order your entries are in, because there's no attempt to connect those entries to form a pattern.

The other four scatter plot options include lines drawn through each plotted point. The two smooth line options try to draw the best curved line between points. The straight line options just connect point 1 to point 2 to point 3 using straight lines between each point. The charts with markers show each of the data points on the line, the charts without markers do not.

PowerPoint draws the line from the first set of coordinates you provide to the second to the third, etc. This introduces a time component into your data since the order you list the data points in impacts the appearance of the line. If you have data where the order of the measurements doesn't matter and you still want to draw a line through the points (like my example of dropping a ball from varying heights where it doesn't matter which height you drop it from first), then you'll want to sort your data by one of the variables before you create your scatter plot.

Here is an example of a scatter plot and a scatter plot with a line for five measurements of the time it takes for a ball dropped from different heights to reach the ground:

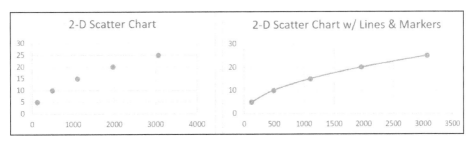

Because I sorted the data before I plotted it, we can see a nice trend line that indicates some sort of exponential relationship exists here.

You can also use scatter plots to chart more than one set of results. You just need to add another column to the provided data table so you can input the values for the second set of results. (The spreadsheet provided by PowerPoint is going to work just like it would in Excel. The only difference is that PowerPoint gives you a data table to start with whereas Excel does not.)

Here is what an X Y or scatter plot looks like with two variables using the different options:

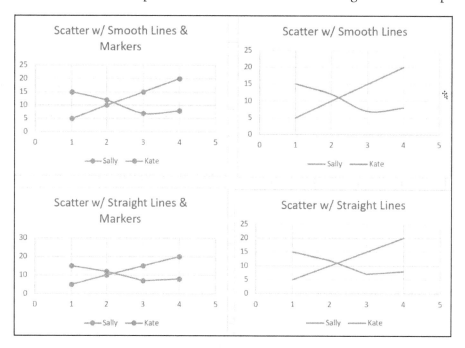

See how the smooth line plots have lines that curve whereas the straight line plots don't? The more drastic the changes between points, the more noticeable that would become.

Note that you can also have multiple results in a basic scatter plot without the lines, but it makes it really hard to tell which is which.

So those are your basic chart types. Now let's talk about how to input the date, edit, and format your charts in PowerPoint.

INSERT A CHART:
DATA, EDITING, AND FORMATTING

Most times when you insert a chart into your presentation you will be dealing with data you already have somewhere else, likely in an Excel spreadsheet. When you insert a chart into PowerPoint, at least in PowerPoint 2013, it gives you a data table with pre-filled values. You can simply type over those values by clicking into the cells in the spreadsheet and replacing with your values. But another option is to copy and paste your data from Excel into the data table provided by PowerPoint.

I did that as an experiment to see how it would work and two things happened. One, it gave me an error message for one of my columns that used a formula, but it was still able to paste in the values that resulted from that formula. And, two, the template table PowerPoint showed had three rows of values but when I pasted in five rows of values the two additional rows of data I pasted into the data table were not visible. They did appear in the chart in the presentation slide, so it was just a formatting issue, but one that it's important to be aware of.

To fix that formatting issue I clicked on the little image of an Excel spreadsheet on the top of the data table so that I could work on the data directly in Microsoft Excel.

From there I was able to just use the format sweeper to make the text I'd added black and therefore visible.

I would highly recommend that if you're going to work with charts in PowerPoint that you become familiar with working with them in Excel. Because basically that's what you're doing. The chart you create just happens to be displayed in PowerPoint.

Now, another option is to just do everything in Excel and then copy and paste the chart you create in Excel into your PowerPoint slide. I just did that and was able to change the colors, fonts, etc. of the pasted chart once it was in PowerPoint. The only difference between the two options is that when you paste from Excel instead of designing your chart in PowerPoint the data behind the chart is stored in that Excel spreadsheet, and any changes to the data that create the chart need to be saved to that Excel spreadsheet. They are not part of the PowerPoint file.

But let's assume you're doing everything in PowerPoint.

You've inserted your chart and now have the chart and data table showing.

To hide the data table, click on the X in the top right corner.

To get the data table back, click on your chart, go to the Data section of the Chart Tools Design tab, and click on the dropdown arrow under Edit Data. You can then either choose Edit Data which will bring back the small data table pane within PowerPoint or you can choose Edit Data in Excel which will open a new Excel file that in my case at least is called Chart in Microsoft Excel.

To change your chart type, click on the chart you've inserted and then click on Change Chart Type in the Type section of the Chart Tools Design tab and select your new chart type from the Change Chart Type dialogue box. Keep in mind when changing chart types that certain chart types, like column and bar charts, are easily interchangeable, but other chart types, like line and pie charts, are not.

To quickly format a chart you can choose from the Chart Styles section of the Chart Tools Design tab which will give you various options with different fills, background, labels, etc. I tend not to like most of the choices, but it can be a good way to get close to what you want and then let you edit from there.

There is also a Quick Layout dropdown menu in the Chart Layouts section of the Chart Tools Design tab. These quick layouts generally involve different label arrangements and data displays.

If you're not too particular about the colors used in your chart, there are a number of pre-formatted color choices under Change Colors in the Chart Styles section of the Chart Tools Design tab.

For more control, you need to look to the Add Chart Element dropdown menu in the Chart Layouts section of the Chart Tools Design tab. You can add, edit, or remove axes, axis titles, chart titles, data labels, data tables, error bars, gridlines, legends, series lines, trendlines, or up/down bars using this dropdown.

For example, I will often add a Data Table with Legend Keys to my charts so that I can see a table of the actual data below my chart. When I do this, I make sure to set the Legend to None because the information is already in the data table.

Also, for pie charts I usually want to include the Data Labels and I usually do so at the Outside End so that I can see what value is represented by each slice in the pie.

This is a good point in time to note that you can also use the formatting panes on the right-hand side to format your chart. To open the formatting panes, right-click on the chart and choose the Format option at the bottom of the dropdown menu. Depending on where you clicked this might be Format Chart Area, Format Data Series, or Format Chart Title, etc. All will open the formatting pane.

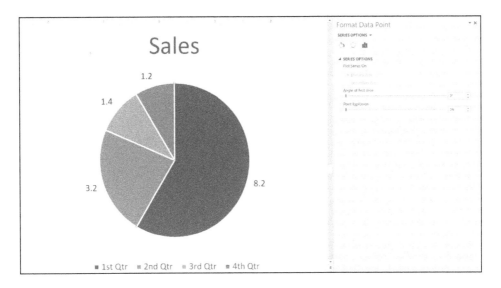

To format other parts of your chart, click on the relevant portion of the chart in your slide and the formatting pane on the right-hand side should change to reflect where you are.

I use the formatting pane when I want to "explode" a pie chart, meaning I want the slices to move outward from one another so that there is space in between each slice. PowerPoint lets you do this slice by slice so that you can pull out one slice from the pie chart and put emphasis on it or it lets you select all of the slices at once and explode all of them outward.

The formatting pane is also where you can rotate the pie chart if it turns out that you want one slice to be at the top instead of in its default position.

To use custom colors in a chart, you can click on each bar, slice, etc. and then go to the Chart Tools Format tab and change the Shape Fill color. Just be sure that when dealing with bar or column charts that all of the related segments are selected before you make your change. This should happen automatically, but sometimes it doesn't. Also, be careful with a pie chart that you don't select all of the slices at once and change them all to the same color.

To use a corporate color choose the More Fill Colors option and then provide the RGB or HSL value for the color you want.

You can also change the fill colors in the formatting pane under the Fill options in the Fill & Line section of the Series Options for Format Data Series.

Next to each chart is a chart filter option. It looks like a little funnel and will let you choose which data points appear in your chart on your slide, so you can have more data in your associated data table than you display.

To format text within a chart you can just select it like normal text and then use the text formatting options in the Font section of the Home tab.

To resize a chart, you can click on the white boxes in the corners or on the sides and drag to the desired size. You can also specify an exact size in the Size section of the Chart Tools Format tab. You can also go to the Format Chart Area pane and in the Size & Properties section under Chart Options you can click on the Size arrow and then specify your values there.

The Format Chart Area pane also includes an option for specifying the exact position of your chart on your slide under the Position option in that same section. Or you can click and drag the chart into position instead.

Okay. Hopefully that gave you a solid overview on working with charts in PowerPoint. As I mentioned before, it's all based on how you'd work with charts in Excel, so if there's ever anything you can't figure out how to do when searching for help in PowerPoint also check Excel's help. And if you're familiar with charts in Excel you should be fine working in PowerPoint and vice versa.

Now on to SmartArt, which is like charts on steroids..

INSERT SMARTART

Time to talk about SmartArt. I'll be honest with you, it was having to talk about SmartArt that kept me from writing this book when I wrote *PowerPoint for Beginners*. It has to be covered in an intermediate guide but I kind of hate it. That's because I've seen it misused far too often and so it annoys me to see it used.

At its best SmartArt allows you to elevate a presentation to another level through the use of slick visual imagery. At its worst SmartArt creates confusion and looks pretentious.

So use it with care and consideration. One of the big mistakes I see with using SmartArt is failing to understand that the graphic in question has a directionality to it or a flow to the numbers.

For example, there is a basic pyramid that you can insert using SmartArt. PowerPoint says you should use this pyramid "to show proportional, interconnected, or hierarchical relationships with the largest component on the bottom and narrowing up." But I have seen this image used to show non-related values on the same slide. I've also seen it used where the largest value was on the top in the smallest segment. And I've also seen where the first two levels of the pyramid were one related set of numbers and the third level was a completely different number.

Do not do that.

Only use SmartArt when it helps others to understand the point you're trying to make. Otherwise, find a different way to present your information.

Okay. Now that the lecture is over, how do you insert SmartArt into a presentation?

One option is to go to the Illustrations section of the Insert tab and click on SmartArt.

Another option is to use a content-type slide and click on the top right image which is for inserting a SmartArt Graphic. (It's the one with a bright-green two-dimensional arrow behind a text box.)

A third option, if you already have your values listed on your slide, is to select those values and then go to the Paragraph section of the Home tab and click on the Convert to SmartArt dropdown arrow and then choose the option you want from there. (I'd usually recommend against using this option because chances are you didn't list your information in the order or format that will work with the SmartArt graphic you want to use and you're probably just better off creating the graphic from scratch. But it's there as an option if you want to try it.)

Okay. So let's say you used the Insert tab and chose SmartArt under the Illustrations section and now you have the Choose a SmartArt Graphic dialogue box showing.

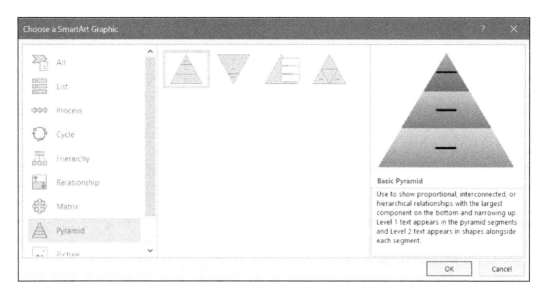

As you click on each possible option in the center of the dialogue box, you will see on the right-hand side of the dialogue box a sample of the graphic and a description of what it should be used for. On the left-hand side of the dialogue box are categories of SmartArt. There are graphics for lists, processes, cycles, hierarchies, relationships, matrices, and pyramids. There is also a section for pictures where you can incorporate a picture into a SmartArt graphic with additional analysis or comment boxes around that picture. And the final option, for Office.com, includes a few additional options.

In other words, you have a lot of options to choose from.

Click on the one you want and then click on OK in the bottom right corner. PowerPoint will then insert a template of that SmartArt graphic into your presentation. If you're using a theme, the colors used for the SmartArt graphic should match the theme you're using.

Here is a basic chevron process flow image. (If you've ever been to business school, you've probably seen this one.)

To customize the text, click on each instance of [Text] and replace it with your own words. The text will resize to fit the image after you hit enter and will do so in all portions of the SmartArt graphic that are of a similar type.

You can see an example of this in the image above. Until I typed in the text for step 3 the other two chevrons had Step 1 and Step 2 in a much larger font size.

To manually change the font size of any of the text boxes, select the text and use the options in the Font section of the Home tab.

When you're dealing with SmartArt you will have additional design and format tabs to work with. Just click on any part of the graphic and look at the top of the screen to see the SmartArt Tools Design and Format tabs.

The Layouts section of the Design tab is where the various SmartArt choices are shown. So if you decide you don't like the graphic you chose, this is where you can change it.

If you want something a little bit fancier than the default appearance, you can do this in the SmartArt Styles section of the Design tab by choosing one of the options from there. For example, on this one I have choices that include a gradient color, beveled edges, and even three-dimensional options.

Let me remind you again that graphics in a presentation should be there to assist you in delivering your message not to distract from the message you're trying to deliver. So while some of these options may be fun or cool or different, always ask yourself if they enhance your presentation or distract from it.

(I know, I'm just a stick in the mud. But remember, most of your bosses and clients probably are, too.)

If you don't like the color used and you're okay with basic color choices, you can use the Change Colors option in the SmartArt Styles section of the SmartArt Tools Design tab to select a choice of basic color schemes.

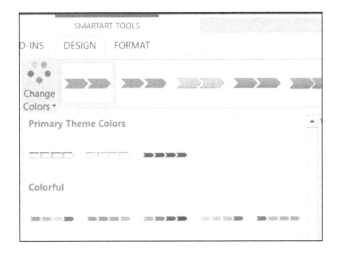

Also, in the Reset section of the Design tab you have an option to convert your SmartArt graphic to text or to reset the graphic back to the default settings that were in place when you inserted it. Both could be very useful under certain circumstances.

If you want to change the order of one of the components in your graphic, then use the Move Up and Move Down options in the Create Graphic section of the Design tab.

So, for example, I can click on the second of my chevrons in the image above, use Move Up, and it will now be the first of the chevrons. The text will move. The color will not.

Clicking on Right to Left will change the direction any arrows are pointing. Clicking on it again will change the arrows back. (Be careful using this one. At least in the U.S. there is an expectation about what direction text and other items flow and having arrows pointing to the left-hand side instead of the right-hand side of the slide is disconcerting. It goes against the natural information flow most people are used to.)

If you want to keep the information from one of your steps in the graphic, but have it turned into a bullet point instead, you can click on it and then use the Demote option in the Create Graphic section of the Design tab.

This is also a short-cut way to add additional items to your graphic. So, for example, I was able to demote one of my steps to a bullet point, then hit enter to get another bullet point, type in the text for that new bullet point, and then Promote both of the bullet points back into the graphic. I then used the Move Up and Move Down options to get them in the order I wanted. What I ended up with was this:

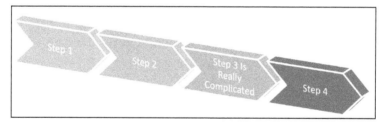

Note that this also uses a different SmartArt Style and one of the options from Change Colors.

Another way to add another step or image to your graphic is to simply click on Add Shape in the top right corner of the Create Graphic section of the Design tab. Then you just have to right-click on the new image, choose Edit Text, and type in your new text. However, I will note that when I added a new step using this method, the text for the individual steps did not automatically resize. So using this approach I would have to go back and manually fix the text to fit each one.

Of course, an easy way to do that if I want to have the same font size for all elements is to use Ctrl + A which will select all of the steps at once and then go to the Home tab and use the Font options there.

Another way to edit your text, and perhaps an easier way, is to select Text Pane under the Create Graphic section of the Design tab. This will bring up a Type Your Text Here dialogue box that will already show bullet points for each item you have in your display.

To add additional items you simply hit Enter at the end of the last item on the list and type your next entry.

This approach does not automatically resize your text for you either, but it is probably the easiest way to add new steps to a SmartArt graphic.

Click on the X in the corner when you're done with the text pane.

You can also bring up the Text Pane by right-clicking somewhere in the area of the SmartArt graphic that is not actually on any component of the graphic and then choosing Show Text Pane from the dropdown menu.

You will very likely need to use the Text Pane when dealing with SmartArt graphics that have more of a flow and hierarchy to them. For example, with the Organization Chart SmartArt graphic it is probably easiest to add new levels of reporting using the Text Pane and indents and bullets. The graphic will adjust as you do so.

You can click on any of the components of the SmartArt graphic and edit them just like you would any shape, but be careful. It's easy to create a mess that way. (If that happens, click on Reset Graphic in the Reset section of the Design tab. You can also right-click on a specific object and Reset Shape or right-click somewhere in the graphic but not on a specific element and Reset Graphic.)

The Format tab under SmartArt Tools should look very familiar because it is basically the same formatting tab you have for shapes. You can change the interior color, the outline, or the shape effects of the items in your SmartArt graphic. This would be one way to apply custom colors to your graphic. Select the shapes that you want to have a specific color and then change it using the Shape Fill option in the Shape Styles section.

You can also open the Format Shape pane, by right-clicking on a shape, choosing Format Shape, and then working from there.

In the Format tab, clicking on the Larger option in the Shapes section will increase the size of all selected shapes. Clicking on the Smaller option will decrease their size.

You can also change the shape that's being used by default in the SmartArt graphic. However, be careful with this one. I selected all and then changed the shape of my rectangular boxes to hexagons, which actually looked pretty nice, but it also changed the lines connecting each box to hexagons as well. To get that effect on just the boxes I had to manually select and change each of the text boxes separately.

This is what it looked like, though:

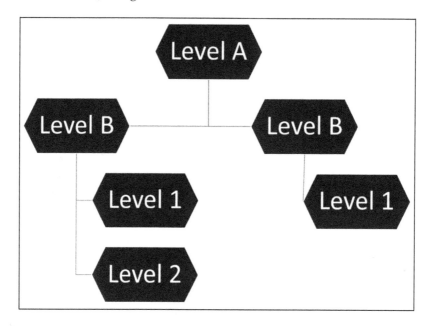

If I'd decided that was a hot mess I could always use Reset Graphic or Ctrl + Z, Undo, as many times as needed.

There are too many types of SmartArt graphic to go through one-by-one here but hopefully you now have a basic understanding of how to select, insert, and edit any of them. Just, please, read the description of their purpose before you use them because it will tell you how the graphic is supposed to be used effectively.

And remember, don't create flows between data points that shouldn't exist, don't mix different sets of data in the same graphic unless the graphic makes it clear that they're different sets, and if there's a hierarchy to the graphic you choose, order your data in line with that hierarchy.

Okay, then. Let's talk something simpler now, inserting a video.

INSERT A VIDEO

I should note here that you may not be able to embed a video in all instances of PowerPoint.

Also, you may not be able to embed it from your desired source if you're using an online source. YouTube should be fine for those versions of PowerPoint that allow you to embed a video (desktop versions of PowerPoint 2013 and later as well as PowerPoint for the web and PowerPoint for Office 365), but other sources may not. Some versions of PowerPoint allow the use of videos from Vimeo and Microsoft Stream, but not all of them.

If you're looking at a blank content slide in PowerPoint 2013 the insert video option is the bottom right option. (Just hold your mouse over it to confirm.) It looks like a snippet of a strip of film with a globe on it.

Click on that image and you should then see an Insert Video dialogue box that is slightly different than the standard dialogue box and is more like when PowerPoint opens access to the internet. It looks like this:

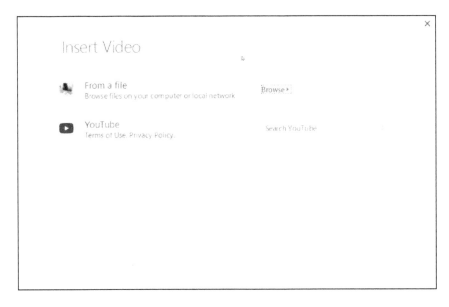

You can also go to the Media section of the Insert tab (at the far right end) and choose the dropdown menu under Video from there. On that dropdown menu you can then choose either Online Video or Video on My PC.

Choosing to insert a video from your PC will open a navigation dialogue box and you can go find the video. Choosing an online video will open a dialogue box similar to the one above but it will only have the two online choices.

If you choose to insert a video from your computer you just need to navigate to where it's saved once the Insert Video dialogue box opens. (This is true for both options.) Select the video from there and then click on Insert.

This will embed the video into your presentation, so keep in mind that this will increase the file size potentially substantially and also that you could lose control over the video if you distribute the PowerPoint file to others. (You still own the copyright, but people are not always good about honoring that.)

Once you insert the video you should then see a still image from the video with play buttons below it.

Click on the play button on the left-hand side to play the video. That button will then turn to a pause button which you can click on if you want to pause the video. There are also volume controls, a time counter, and the ability to move forward or backward .25 seconds at a time.

To delete the video, just click on it and then use the Delete key.

When you navigate away from the slide with the video on it and come back to it, you may not see the play button below the video but move your mouse over the image and you will then see it. When you are presenting your slides, the play bar will be on the bottom edge of the image instead of below it.

If the video is not on your computer, you can insert a video from online. There is a specific option for YouTube videos as well as the ability to embed a video from a video embed code. At least in PowerPoint 2013, these are both for YouTube.

If you choose the YouTube option then you will be able to search for the video you want on YouTube. Searching for a set of terms brings up relevant results and thumbnail images.

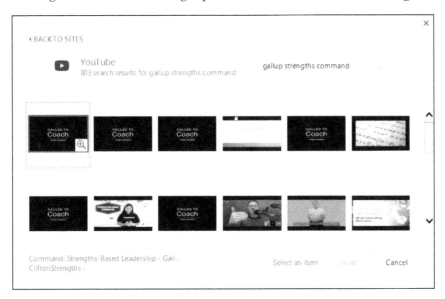

You can then hold your mouse over each one to see the full description of the video. Click on the video you want and then choose Insert.

You can also embed a YouTube video using the video embed code option. To do that you need to go to YouTube to obtain the embed code. Be sure it starts with <iframe and ends with </iframe>. An embed code that uses http: will not work.

You can resize the associated image that's inserted by clicking on the white boxes in the corners and dragging.

To preview an online video you need to right-click on the video image and choose Preview from the dropdown menu. Or you can go to the Video Tools Playback tab and choose Play from the Preview section there. In both instances this will show a YouTube play button in the center of the video and you can then click on that play button to watch the video. This is loading from the internet, so should not work if you are not connected to the internet.

This will be true when you present as well. To play a video you have inserted from online you need an internet connection and, at least in PowerPoint 2013, access to Internet Explorer 9 (MS12-037) or Internet Explorer 10 or later. This also only works with the desktop version of PowerPoint, not the online version.

Also, it appears that playing online videos may be glitchy in certain versions of PowerPoint. So be careful if you rely on this as an option and don't have control over the version of PowerPoint or the computer that will be used during the presentation. (You can always hyperlink to a video instead if you can't manage to embed a video in your presentation.)

Once you embed an external video in your presentation there may also be a warning message the next time you open the presentation about external media objects. If so, you'll need to Enable Content for it to work.

Okay. So you have a video that you've inserted into your presentation. Now what?

Click on the video and you should see two new tabs in the menu bar under Video Tools. One is Format and one is Playback.

In the Format tab you can fix the brightness/contrast in the video, change its coloring, add a poster frame around the edges, change the video screen shape from a rectangle to any of the available shapes, make the border around the image any color you want, and add special effects to the border.

Those special border effects will go away as soon as the video starts playing if it's an embedded YouTube video but not if it's your own embedded video.

In the Format tab you can also specify an exact size for the video in the Size section.

In the Video Options section of the Playback tab you can specify whether the video should start automatically or when you click on it using the Start dropdown menu.

You can also say whether to hide the video when it's not playing and whether to rewind after playing by checking the respective boxes in that same section.

If the video is one you have embedded (so your own video) then on the Playback tab you have more options. You can add a bookmark at a specific point in the video, you can trim the video so that only a portion of it will play when clicked, you can add a fade in or fade out effect, you can set the video to play on full screen, and you can set it to play on a continuous loop until stopped.

For the most part I'd avoid using those options. I tried the fade in and was not very impressed by it. The Trim Video option in the Editing section is convenient if you have raw video footage and no other way to trim it, but it's probably best to do those sorts of things outside of the program since the size of your video file will impact the size of your presentation file.

INSERT ONLINE PICTURES

In *PowerPoint for Beginners* we covered how to insert a picture into a presentation, but there's another option that PowerPoint offers and that's to insert an *online* picture.

It's one of the six options shown on a content side. In this case it's the middle option in the bottom row and it looks like a picture with a globe in the bottom right corner.

You can also go to the Images section of the Insert tab and choose Online Pictures from there.

Clicking on either option will bring up a web-based dialogue box that allows you to either search Bing or to find an image in your OneDrive account.

When I searched for cute pandas the results defaulted to images that were available under a creative commons license. (This generally means you can use those images with the permission of the image owner.) I would be very cautious before I unchecked that box and used an image that wasn't under that kind of license, because it is a violation of copyright to use an image you don't have the right to use and it can get you sued and cost you money.

This is what the search box looks like:

When you click on an image it is downloaded and inserted into your presentation. You can then resize the image by clicking on it and going to the Picture Tools Format tab.

(Based on the Help text for this feature it appears that there are additional online search options available in later versions of PowerPoint, but the process should be basically the same.)

This is also how you now insert clip art into a presentation. It is no longer built into PowerPoint.

You can also add borders and adjust the image through the Picture Tools Format tab or by right-clicking on the image, choosing Format Picture, and then working in the Format Picture pane on the right-hand side.

INSERT PHOTO ALBUM

It's not an option available on a content slide, because it's actually creating a new presentation, but PowerPoint does also give you the option to "insert a photo album".

To do so you need to go to the Insert tab and choose Photo Album from the Images section. There's a dropdown menu there and the only option available (if you haven't already inserted a photo album) will be New Photo Album.

Select this option and it will bring up the Photo Album dialogue box.

Click on File/Disk under Insert Picture From on the left-hand side which will bring up an Insert New Pictures dialogue box.

Mine by default opened to my Pictures folder. Navigate to where the photos you want to use are stored and either select them one-by-one and choose Insert or check the top left corner of each one you want (assuming they're all in the same location) and then choose Insert to insert them all at once.

You'll now have a listing of the photos you've chosen with a preview image of the currently selected image on the right-hand side of the dialogue box.

You can insert a text box into the photo album by clicking on New Text Box, but you'll need to wait until you generate the photo album to add the actual text. Note that when you do this, the text will appear on its own slide, not below the image.

You can choose to make all of the pictures in the album black and white instead of color by checking the appropriate box on the left-hand side of the Photo Album dialogue box.

You can also set the album layout by using the dropdowns at the bottom of the dialogue box.

Choosing Fit To Slide will size each picture so that either the height or width fills the entire slide, depending on which edge is reached first.

Choosing 1 Picture will show one picture per slide but the picture will have about an inch of space on the outer edge that's the closest to the border. When you choose this option it also allows you to check the box to have a caption below each image which will by default be the image name.

Like so:

IMG_0912 - Copy

(I should note here that when I first generated the photo album the background was black not white, but because these will be printed in a book at some point I changed that by choosing a different Theme in the Design tab.)

Choosing 2 Pictures will put two pictures per slide with enough room for a caption. Choosing 4 Pictures will put four pictures per slide.

Choosing the "with title" options (for example, 1 Picture with Title) will include a title bar at the top of the slide with the number of specified images below that.

By default the images will be inserted in the presentation as a basic rectangle shape, but you can also change that by choosing a different shape from the Frame Shape dropdown. Your choices are rectangle, rounded rectangle, simple frame white, simple frame black, compound frame black, center shadow rectangle, and soft edge rectangle.

The easiest way to test what you want is to make your choice, choose Update, and see what it looks like, and then if that's not what you wanted go back to the Insert tab and choose Edit Photo Album from the Photo Album dropdown in the Images section and change to a different choice.

You can also get into the Edit Photo Album dialogue box by right-clicking on one of the slide thumbnails in the left-hand navigation pane and choosing Photo Album from the dropdown menu.

The Photo Album dialogue box also lets you set the Theme to use before you generate the picture album, but since I don't have the names of the different themes memorized it was easier for me to just choose a theme after I'd generated my picture album by going to the Design tab instead.

If you make changes in the presentation itself instead of using the photo album dialogue box there is a warning that your changes could be lost if you then update the picture album through the dialogue box, so be careful of that. It's probably best to use the dialogue box to start the photo album and then do the rest in the presentation itself without re-opening the dialogue box.

MASTER SLIDES:
JUST A QUICK NOTE

Alright...

So we just covered a number of items you can insert into a presentation.

Now we need to talk about master slides.

They can be dangerous to mess with, which is why I've held off on talking about them to this point, but you're bound to have thought about them. For example, you might have thought, "How do I get this color I'm putting into the title section on all of my slides at once?"

One answer is that you can do that through making edits to your master slides.

(Another answer is to select multiple slides at once in the left-hand navigation pane and then the edits you make on that one slide will carry through to the others that you selected. The reason the master slide option may be better is that it will also apply to new slides you insert into the presentation.)

I would recommend that if you're going to make changes to the master slides that you do so before you start to build your presentation. Otherwise you're liable to have text that isn't fully visible or situations where some images or backgrounds update to show the changes you made and others don't.

To see your master slides, go to the Master Views section of the View tab, and click on the Slide Master option.

It will take you to the master slide for the type of content slide you were on at the time. If you look in the left-hand navigation pane you'll see all master slides for your presentation, not just that one.

If you want a change to apply to all slide types, then click on the very top thumbnail image in the left-hand pane.

If not, you can click on just that one specific slide type and edit it instead, but then the changes you make will only apply to that slide type.

Honestly, we're on the edge of advanced PowerPoint here so I'm not going to go into too much more detail on this, but I did want you to know this option existed in case you needed it. You can really mess things up fast by mucking around in your master slides, so do so with extreme caution.

CHANGING THE BACKGROUND OF
ALL SLIDES AT ONCE

As I alluded to above, there are other ways to change multiple slides at once. So let's walk through how to change the background of all of your slides at once without changing the slide master.

One option is to click onto a slide and then click on the Format Background option under the Customize section of the Design tab. This will bring up the Format Background pane on the right-hand side of the screen. Change the background to what you want it to look like and then click on the Apply to All button at the bottom of the pane.

You can also, of course, open the Format Background pane by right-clicking on the outer edge of a slide and choosing Format Background from the dropdown menu.

If you only want to apply a different background to some of your slides, but not all of them, you can select those slides in the left-hand navigation pane. Click on your first slide, hold down the Ctrl key, click on the remainder of the slides you want to include, and then go through the same steps with the Format Background option in the Design tab. Your changes should show on all selected slides.

This method of selecting multiple slides also works for other slide-level edits like adding a color to the title section of a slide or adding a footer to the slide.

SELECT ALL

You can select all of your slides or all of the objects on a slide using the Select All option. The easiest way to use Select All is through the control shortcut, Ctrl + A. Click into the text box on the slide where you want to select all of the text, or onto the slide where you want to select all of the objects, or on a slide thumbnail image in the left-hand navigation pane and then use Ctrl + A.

For text the text will be highlighted in gray. For objects you'll see boxes around each shape/image. For slides you'll see a red border around each slide thumbnail image in the navigation pane.

You can then, for example, format all of the text at once with a new font, move all of the selected objects, or copy all of the slides at once.

Another option for selecting all is to go to the Editing section of the Home tab and then choose Select All or Select Objects from the dropdown menu.

(As we discussed previously the third option in that dropdown, Selection Pane, lets you see all of the objects on a slide and select just the ones you want by using Ctrl or Shift and clicking on items listed in that pane.)

SECTIONS

You can also split a presentation into multiple sections. PowerPoint recommends doing this to allocate tasks between team members, for example. It also makes it easier to move slides around because you can collapse a section and then click and drag that whole section to a new location in the presentation.

If you have a very lengthy presentation it can make navigating the presentation a lot easier if you use sections. You can have each main section of the presentation be a section and then collapse those sections so that you only see the slides for the section you're working on. Like so:

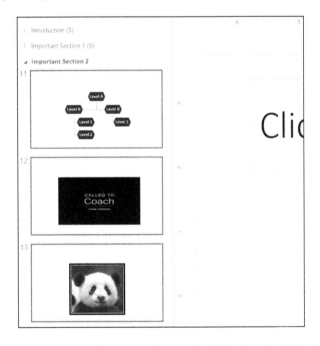

To insert a section, right-click onto the space above the slide thumbnail in the left-hand navigation pane where you want to start your new section and choose Add Section. This will insert a new section starting with that slide.

Initially, the section will be named Untitled Section.

To rename the section, right-click on the name, choose Rename Section from the dropdown menu, type in the name you want in the Rename Section dialogue box, and then click on Rename.

When you right-click on a section name you can see that you have other options related to sections.

You can remove that section (but keep the slides), remove the section and its slides, remove all of the sections in the presentation (but keep the slides), move the section up (if possible), move the section down (if possible), collapse all of the sections in the presentation (so all slides in sections are hidden), or expand all of the sections (so all slides are visible). Just right-click on the section name and choose the option you want.

These options are also available in the Slide section of the Home tab under the Section dropdown menu..

COMMENTS

If you're working with others on drafting a presentation you may at some point want to add a comment to the presentation so that those others can see it but it's not part of the actual presentation.

To do this, go to the point in the presentation where you want to make the comment, click onto that location, and then go to the Comments section of the Review tab, and click on New Comment. This will open the Comments pane on the right-hand side and show your user name and a white text box where you can type in your comment.

Each comment will show who made it and when.

When there is a comment on a slide, it will show as a small quote bubble in a peach-sort of color. You can click on this quote bubble to show the Comments pane. If you don't want to go searching for a comment bubble to make this happen, you can also just go to the Show Comments dropdown in the Comments section of the Review tab and make sure that Comments Pane is checked. This too will bring up the Comments pane on the right-hand side of the screen.

To navigate between comments either use the Previous and Next options in the Comments section of the Review tab or at the top of the Comments pane. At the top of the Comments pane these options are not labeled with text, but they show as icons of pieces of paper with arrows pointing either to the right or the left.

To reply to an existing comment you can type into the white text box directly below the comment which says "Reply…" in gray letters. (A nice thing to have that didn't used to exist.)

You can also make a new comment in response but that's the old way and a messier option that sometimes doesn't maintain the thread of the conversation as well.

To edit an existing comment, click on the text and it will become a white text box and you can then add to, delete, or edit the text.

If you use comments, always be sure to delete them before the final version is saved. To do this, go to the Comments section of the Review tab, click on the Delete dropdown, and choose the Delete All Comments and Ink in This Presentation option.

(You can also make sure this is done by going to the File tab and then choosing Check For Issues under Inspect Presentation in the Info section.)

INCORPORATING
GROUP EDITS

Unlike Word, PowerPoint does not have a track changes option, at least not in PowerPoint 2013. What they recommend doing instead is to save the original draft of your presentation and then save a renamed version of the presentation and make that renamed version available for people to add their comments or make their edits through a share site. Once those edits or comments have been made to the second version of the presentation you can then bring them into the original version of the presentation and review them by using the Compare function.

So let's walk through how to do that.

To compare two presentations, open the original version of the presentation in PowerPoint, go to the Compare section of the Review tab, and click on Compare.

This will open the Choose File to Merge with Current Presentation dialogue box. Navigate to where you have the second version of the presentation saved, select it, and then click on the Merge button.

You will now see your initial presentation with a Revisions pane on the right-hand side. If there are no edits to the current slide it will tell you so and then tell you the next slide which does have edits.

If there are also comments in the merged presentation you will see the Comments pane on the right-hand side as well. If there are no comments in the current slide it will say so but there will be previous and next navigation options to move to the next comment in the presentation.

For changes that were made to the presentation itself you can either navigate to the specified slide using the thumbnails in the navigation pane on the left-hand side of the screen or go to the Compare section of the Review tab and use the Next option.

For comments, you can use the previous and next buttons in the Comments pane or the Previous and Next options in the Comments section of the Review tab.

Note, however, that the different options may take you to different edits.

For example, I had made background changes to some of the slides in the presentation. The Review pane told me that there were edits on the 3rd slide and when I went to that slide the edit shown was a background edit. But when I used the Next option from the Compare section of the Review tab it instead showed me a high-level background edit affecting multiple slides.

Now, here's where it gets weird.

The view of the current slide as you see it on the screen is how it existed in your original version. To see how it looks with the identified edits, click on the small image showing a piece of paper with a pencil in the top right corner of the slide. That will then show a description of the edit(s). Click on the box next to the edit description to then show the edit on the slide.

Here is what the box and the description look like. The box to click is where the arrow is:

To remove the edit from your view, uncheck that box.

When the change is not visible, you can accept it. You do this by going to the Compare section of the Review tab, clicking on the Accept dropdown option, and then choosing Accept Change. This will then make the edit visible and you will have accepted it.

(Who came up with that, I do not know. It's very counterintuitive in my opinion.)

When the change is visible, you can reject it. So you check the little box to see the edit and only then will you have the Reject option in the Compare section of the Review tab. To reject a change, click on the dropdown under Reject, and choose Reject Change. The change will then go away and you will have officially rejected it.

Like I said, very backwards to my way of thinking.

For changes that involve moving a slide to a new location, those will be shown in the left-hand navigation pane.

The slide that was moved will have the little icon of a page with a pencil in the top right corner of the thumbnail. If you hold your mouse over the icon, it will tell you where the slide was moved to in the new version. It will be in the old position when you do this.

Any slide that has been moved will also be listed as having changes in the Presentation Changes box in the right-hand Revisions pane. However, if there are no other changes, the Slide Changes detail box will show no information.

Presentation Changes

- Presentation properties
- Theme (1 · 14)
- Slides moved after Slide 5
- Slide 11
- Slide 12: The Baker Valley
- Slide 13
- Slide 14

If slides were moved as a group then the Presentation Changes box will also have an entry along the lines of "slides moved after Slide 14" and when you click on that there will be a small description displayed in the navigation pane on the left-hand side showing a listing of all of the slides that were moved.

To accept a change in the left-hand navigation pane, right-click on the image that indicates a change and choose Accept Change. To reject a change in the left-hand navigation pane, you have to check the box to show the change, and then right-click and Reject Change.

Honestly, I find this a very awkward way to review changes in a presentation. If I were faced with a situation like this what I would likely do, assuming I trusted my team not to make crazy edits that I needed to know about, would be to immediately accept all of the changes in the presentation and then review the presentation as if it was supposed to be a final version. (Which is basically just reviewing the second version of the presentation without ever having to Compare the two versions which is the old way of doing things.)

Compare is nice in the sense that it will keep you from missing any changes that were made that can slip by. But it's really messy how they've set it up. At least you know it exists now and what its quirks are in case you want to use it..

ZOOM AND VIEWS

We've pretty much covered the big ticket items you need to know to work at an intermediate level in PowerPoint, but I wanted to cover a few little clean up items before we wrap up.

First, let's look at how to use Zoom and what the different Views options are.

On occasion, you may want to increase the size of the slide you're viewing or you may want to decrease its size. This can be done using Zoom.

To do this, go to the Zoom section of the View tab and click on Zoom. This will bring up the Zoom dialogue box. By default my slides are set at 85%. You can change that number or you can click the white circle next to one of the pre-selected values which are 400%, 200%, 100%, 66%, 50%, and 33%.

Choosing a value that is greater than your current value will make the slide on your screen larger. Choosing a value that is less than your current value will make it smaller. The panes on either side will not change size.

If you zoom to the point where you can't see the entire slide then scroll bars will appear on the bottom and right side of the slide image so that you can scroll to see the entire slide.

In that same Zoom section of the View tab there is also a Fit to Window option. Click on it to return to the standard zoom level of 85%.

According to PowerPoint if you want "zoomier zooming" you can use the controls in the status bar. That's in the bottom right corner of the screen. You'll see a slider with a negative sign on one side, a plus sign on the other side, and 85% (or whatever your current zoom level is) next to the plus sign. To zoom using this option, click on the wide solid white bar that is perpendicular to that line and located somewhere between the plus and minus signs and then drag either left to zoom out or right to zoom in. The very thin white mark that is perpendicular to that line represents the 100% mark.

You can also click on the plus and minus marks at either end of the line to move up or down to the nearest 10% mark. So originally you'll move from 85% to 80% or 90% but then you'll move to 70% or 100% and so on.

* * *

Another trick to be aware of is that you can change your default slide view if you want. This is done by selecting one of the options in the Presentation Views section of the View tab.

The default, or Normal, view shows the one slide that you're currently on in the center of the screen with a navigation pane on the left-hand side that contains thumbnails of the other slides in your presentation. If you have notes on your presentation, those will appear at the bottom.

Outline View, the next option, replaces the thumbnails in the presentation with the text from each slide shown in a bulleted or list format. You can click on that text and delete, edit, or add to it but not format it. In this view, the current presentation slide is still visible on the right half of the screen, but it's smaller. The notes section below the slide remains.

According to PowerPoint "[w]orking in Outline view is particularly handy if you want to make global edits, get an overview of your presentation, change the sequence of bullets or slides, or apply formatting changes."

They also say that you can easily create an entire presentation by pasting your outline from Word into the Outline pane. I tried this and it just put all of the text into one slide. However, when I went looking for how to actually do this I did find a way to use a Word outline to create your slides, so let's cover it here very quickly.

First, in your Word document you need to use Styles to assign your text as Heading 1, Heading 2, Heading 3, etc. Heading 1 will be your slide title, Heading 2 will be the first-level bullet point, Heading 3 will be the second-level bullet point, etc.

Save your Word document and close it. Now go to the Slides section of the Home tab, click on New Slide, and choose Slides from Outline. Navigate to where your Word file is saved, select it, and choose Open. PowerPoint will use your Word outline to create a series of slides in your presentation. If you happen to have your information written this way already, it's a very easy way to get your text into your presentation.

Okay. Now the next view.

The Slide Sorter view shows you thumbnails of all of your slides but no central slide to edit. This is probably the most useful view for moving slides around within your presentation. The big advantage of this view over the Normal view is that you have more slides visible. Combine this view with Zoom Out and you can see approximately seventy slides at once.

To move a slide, left-click and drag it to where you want it. When you do this, all other slides will move over to accommodate the slide you moved.

You can also select multiple slides by clicking on one slide and then either holding down Ctrl and clicking on individual slides or Shift and clicking on the first or last slide in the series you want to select. Once your slides are selected, left-click and drag the entire set of selected slides to their new location.

Rather than click and drag the slides you can also use Copy (Ctrl +C) or Cut (Ctrl + X) and Paste (Ctrl + V) to move the slides around.

The next view, the Notes Page view, will show you the slide and any notes for that slide as they will appear when printed. You can actually click into the text box for the notes in this view and add notes or edit notes.

(If all you want is to know what notes you have on a slide, the easier option is to stay in the Normal view and just click on Notes in the status bar at the bottom of the screen. Click on Notes again to hide your notes from view.)

The final view, the Reading View, shows you how the slide will look as part of a presentation, including any animations and transitions, without requiring that you view it as a full screen presentation.

In this view, you can use the arrows in the status bar at the bottom to move forward or backward through the presentation. You can also just click on the slide to move forward. Or use the arrow keys on your keyboard.

Use Esc or left-click on Menu (which is between the two arrows in the status bar) and choose End Show to get back to the normal PowerPoint screen. You can also click on the Normal icon in the status bar next to the right arrow to get back to the Normal View.

So those are your views. I usually just work in the Normal View, but each has its potential value.

SAVE AS PDF

I covered how to save a file and how to change the format of that file when you save it in *PowerPoint for Beginners*, but there are a few extra tips I wanted to share about saving a PowerPoint presentation as a PDF.

To save a PowerPoint presentation as a PDF file choose the Save As option and then in the Save As Type dropdown menu choose PDF (*.pdf) and click on Save. This will create a single PDF file with one page per presentation slide.

But there are other PDF options available to you. To see them, choose Save As, select PDF (*.pdf) from the dropdown menu, but then click on Options.

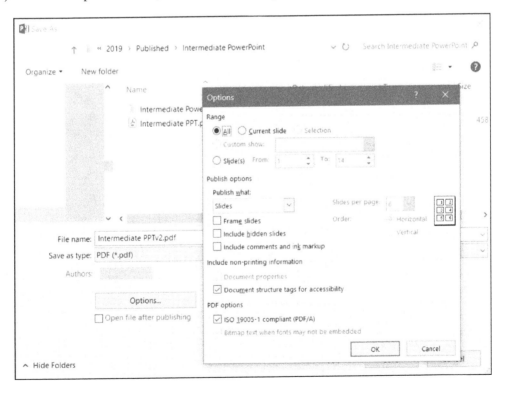

From here you can make a number of choices.

If you just want the current slide to be saved as a PDF, click on Current Slide in the first row of options under Range.

If you want to save a set of slides but not the entire presentation as a PDF, use the Slide(s) option in the Range section and then type in the first slide number and last slide number for your range of slides.

If the slides you want to save are not continuous, then select them first using Ctrl and the navigation pane and then when you choose to Save As a PDF, use the Selection choice from the Range section. This will save your selected slides as a single PDF file.

You can also create a PDF of the handouts version of your presentation, the notes pages from the presentation, or the outline view of the presentation using the Publish What dropdown in the Publish options section of the Options dialogue box. Choosing handouts will let you specify the number of slides to include on each printed page.

Another way to generate a PDF file is by using the Export and then Create a PDF/XPS Document option under the Home tab. It brings up the same dialogue box but with the PDF file type already selected. The Options button is also available, but in a slightly different location.

SAVE AS JPG, PNG, OR GIF

Another Save As option that I've used on occasion was the ability to save my presentation as images. This is because in the past I've used PowerPoint to create the images that I placed in my books. I would paste the screenshot I intended to use into a PowerPoint slide, add arrows and text, trim the image, and then export the result as a .jpg image I could insert into my presentation.

To generate image files from your PowerPoint presentation, choose Save As and then select GIF Graphics Interchange Format (*.gif), JPEG File Interchange Format (*.jpg), or PNG Portable Network Graphics Format (*.png) from the Save As Type dropdown menu. Which image type you prefer is up to you. I usually use a .jpg file but that's more personal preference than reasoned decision making.

Once you do this, PowerPoint is going to ask you, "Which slides do you want to export?" If you choose All Slides it will create a new folder using the name you have the presentation saved under and will then save each individual slide as its own image file within that folder. It will name those files according to their slide number. So you'll have a folder named, for example, Intermediate PowerPoint with files inside it named Slide1.GIF, Slide2.GIF, etc.

If you choose Just This One instead PowerPoint will save just the current slide as an image file using with the name of the presentation. So I might end up with Intermediate PowerPoint.jpg and that would be one slide from the presentation Intermediate PowerPoint that is saved as a JPG image.

SLIDE TRANSITIONS

In *PowerPoint for Beginners* I covered how to use animations to have only a portion of the text on a slide appear at a time. This can be very useful when doing a presentation so that the people you're talking to don't read ahead and stop listening to you.

I tend to have a strong dislike for most of the animations options where text spins onto the screen or wheels in or grows and turns, etc. It's usually not necessary and distracts from what you're trying to do.

Which is why I didn't cover the equivalent for slides, which are called Transitions. I'd generally recommend against using these, but they exist and if you feel you must...

To add a transition from one slide to the next, click on the slide in the left-hand pane that you want to transition to and then go to the Transitions tab and click on the transition type you want to use from the Transition To This Slide section.

As you click on your choice, PowerPoint will briefly show the transition in the main view portion of the screen. So you will see the prior slide transitioning to your current one using the selected transition type. By default the transition will take one second.

If you miss this demonstration or want to see it again, you can click on the Preview option on the left-hand side of the Transitions tab and it will run again.

If you want the transition to take longer, this can be adjusted in the Timing section of the Transitions tab by changing the Duration.

If you want all of your slides to have the same transition settings that you've already applied to the current slide (duration, sound, type), click on Apply To All in the Timing section of the Transitions tab.

If you really want to annoy people, you can even add a sound to your slide transition. This is also under the Timing section of the Transitions tab. Choose the sound you want from the Sound dropdown. The sound will then play as the slide transitions. If you choose just a sound transition but no movement, you'll need to run the slide show or use the Reading View to hear it in action.

The Transitions tab is also where you can change the setting that advances a presentation to the next slide using a mouse click. You can also or instead set it to advance after a set period of time under the Advance Slide settings in the Timing section.

Again, to see this one in action, you'll need to launch the slide show or use the Reading View.

To apply the same timing to all of your slides, select them all first, and then specify the setting you want to use or check Apply to All when you're done.

(I will note here that setting it to have a one second delay and using the bomb sound effect looked like it would be very effective for a presentation of horrific battlefield images or something like that, so it's not that there's never a use for these settings. It's just that you need to be careful that you use them appropriately. Remember, if it doesn't enhance the point you're trying to get across, then you probably shouldn't do it.)

CONCLUSION

Alright. That's it.

Hopefully you now have a better understanding of PowerPoint than you did when you started. However, as the name implies, this was not meant to be a comprehensive guide to PowerPoint. The basics of using PowerPoint were already covered in *PowerPoint for Beginners* and there are some more advanced skills I didn't mention here at all or that I mentioned enough for you to know about but not in full and complete detail.

But at this point I hope you've learned enough about how PowerPoint works that you can find those additional answers on your own. PowerPoint, like all of Office, tends to follow a certain logic so that when you don't know how to do something you can often figure it out based on how you did other similar tasks.

But there are also a number of excellent help options out there to assist you.

The first option is to left-click on the small question mark in the top right corner of PowerPoint or use F1 to launch the PowerPoint Help dialogue box.

There will be some popular categories listed as well as a search box where you can type in what you're looking for. Using PowerPoint help will often lead you to the answer you need.

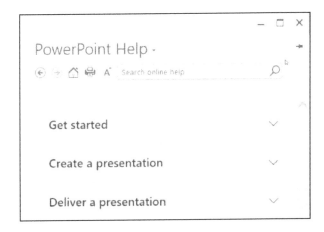

Within PowerPoint some of the menu choices also have a basic description which you can see if you just hold your mouse over them. In addition, some of those descriptions include a Tell Me More note at the bottom that you can click on to launch the specific help description for that option.

For example, if I go to the Text section of the Insert tab and hold my mouse over the WordArt dropdown it tells me that I can "add some artistic flair to my document using a WordArt text box" and then has Tell Me More at the bottom. If I click on that Tell Me More it takes me straight to the help section for Insert WordArt.

Be aware that a number of the help topics in PowerPoint 2013 also will automatically launch a video. If you like videos, great. If not, close the video and you'll still have the help box with a text description.

If the help options within PowerPoint are not enough, you can also do an internet search to find your answer. Be sure to include the version of PowerPoint you're working in and some keywords that are relevant to your search. I usually choose the support.office.com results first because I expect them to be the most official and reliable option. But if it's a "can you do this weird thing" question as opposed to a "how does this work" question, then sometimes you'll need to branch out to other sources.

Worst case scenario, there are a number of online user forums where you can ask a question. I tend to avoid these because they seem to attract very rude and opinionated people who will tell you that you didn't ask the question properly instead of just asking politely for more information. But a lot of times on those forums someone else will have already asked your question and you can just sort through to find the answer they were given.

Also, you're always welcome to reach out to me. Chances are I'll know the answer or be able to find it for you easily enough. Just send an email.

And that's that. Remember, the goal of a presentation is usually to convey information so if whatever you're trying to do with your presentation doesn't accomplish that, then don't do it. PowerPoint is tremendously powerful and gives you all sorts of options, but that can be a danger as much as a help. So keep it as clean and simple as you can. Don't let the appearance overwhelm the message.

Good luck with it.

INDEX

ABOUT THE AUTHOR

M.L. Humphrey is a former stockbroker with a degree in Economics from Stanford and an MBA from Wharton who has spent close to twenty years as a regulator and consultant in the financial services industry.

You can reach M.L. at mlhumphreywriter@gmail.com or at mlhumphrey.com.

www.ingramcontent.com/pod-product-compliance
Lightning Source LLC
LaVergne TN
LVHW082035050326
832904LV00005B/178